The Jesus Bible

SAVIOR

THE STORY OF GOD'S RESCUE PLAN

Aaron Coe, Ph.D.
Series Writer & General Editor of *The Jesus Bible*

Matt Rogers, Ph.D.
Series Writer & Lead Writer of *The Jesus Bible*

Harper*Christian* Resources

passionpublishing

The Jesus Bible Study Series: Savior
© 2023 by Passion Publishing

Published in Grand Rapids, Michigan, by HarperChristian Resources. HarperChristian Resources is a registered trademark of HarperCollins Christian Publishing, Inc.

Requests for information should be sent to customercare@harpercollins.com.

ISBN 978-0-310-15504-1 (softcover)
ISBN 978-0-310-15505-8 (ebook)

HarperChristian Resources titles may be purchased in bulk for church, business, fundraising, or ministry use. For information, please e-mail ResourceSpecialist@ChurchSource.com.

First printing December 2023 / Printed in the United States of America

CONTENTS

Introduction v

Lesson 1: **God with Us** 1

Lesson 2: **God-Man** 15

Lesson 3: **Mission** 31

Lesson 4: **Kingdom** 47

Lesson 5: **Saved** 63

Lesson 6: **Alive** 77

Leader's Guide 93

About the Authors 97

INTRODUCTION

Every story inevitably reaches a climactic juncture—that pivotal moment when the mounting tension between the protagonist and antagonist demands resolution. It is the point at which a solution to the looming problem must be confronted and a path forward must be charted. In our ongoing journey through *The Jesus Bible Study Series*, we find ourselves at this very juncture.

Throughout this series, we have explored the Creation narrative, where God formed the world and, within this grand design, humanity made its entrance. We have delved into the narrative of humankind's rebellion against God's perfect plan—an uprising that severed the bond between humanity and its Creator. We then witnessed God's selection of Israel as a key player in his redemptive process . . . yet we also learned that the ultimate fulfillment of this redemption had not yet been realized.

It was against this tapestry of Israel's history that God began to unveil his blueprint for a Savior who would manifest as the embodiment of his divine plan. This Messiah, once and for all, would bridge the chasm between humanity and God for those who believed in him. He would descend on the world as both fully divine and fully human, becoming the ultimate atonement for the sins of humanity.

From the inception of God's divine plan, a Savior had been the integral component. Jesus was, so to speak, God's "Plan A" from the very outset. He arrived on earth at an appointed time and place, driven by a precise purpose. In his divinity, Jesus performed miracles and forgave sins, while in his humanity, he empathized with the struggles of humankind. He was the perfect, and only, God-man.

Jesus, the Savior of humanity, was not an abstract concept. He physically descended to earth and fully embraced our human messiness, even unto death. In the end, he triumphed over death and rose from the grave. This account might seem like a fairy tale were it not grounded in the tangible reality of a specific time and place—a place we can visit even today—among real individuals who left us their eyewitness testimonies. We can bear witness to the locations where Jesus resided. We can read firsthand accounts of the wondrous events that transpired during his years on earth. This undeniable reality should instill in us a profound confidence that our faith is not a work of fantasy but rather a vibrant and authentic force.

As a reminder, *Savior* is the fourth of six "acts" in God's beautiful overarching story told throughout Scripture: (1) **Beginnings**, (2) **Revolt**, (3) **People**, (4) **Savior**, (5) **Church**, (6) **Forever**. Every detail in each story found within the pages of the Bible could be placed within one of these six acts, which tell God's story from Genesis to Revelation. In this act, *Savior,* you will delve into the person of Jesus. *Savior* will help you comprehend why Jesus stands as the fulfillment of God's ultimate design, and you will come to recognize and grasp the profound truth that he is "God with us." Jesus is not only the wellspring of your salvation but also the catalyst of a specific mission for your life. His intent was never solely to secure your heavenly destiny (though that is undoubtedly part of it) but rather to empower you to live out his divine purpose on earth and, in doing so, bring him glory.

As we embark on this journey together, our prayer is that you encounter Jesus in a profound way. We pray that as you behold him, your faith will be deepened. We pray that your life will be enriched and infused with a greater sense of purpose in your day-to-day existence. We pray for the strengthening of your relationships and for the flourishing of the church, all catalyzed by a deeper and more profound encounter with Jesus, the Savior of the world.

—Aaron & Matt

Lesson One

GOD WITH US

"Therefore the Lord himself will give you a sign:
The virgin will conceive and give birth to a son, and will
call him Immanuel."

ISAIAH 7:14

The Word became flesh and made his dwelling among us.
We have seen his glory, the glory of the one and only
Son, who came from the Father, full of grace and truth.

JOHN 1:14

The LORD your God
is with you,
The Mighty Warrior
who saves.

ZEPHANIAH 3:17

WELCOME

Streaming something on television or online is okay. Reading about a place in a book is good and can even be exciting. Watching a movie can certainly be fun. But nothing can replace the real thing. Nothing can compare to seeing—firsthand—that person, place, or thing you had previously only experienced in a two-dimensional form. Why? Because *seeing is believing*.

When my (Aaron's) four kids were younger, they loved all the Disney characters and movies. My youngest daughter, Harper, especially loved Anna and Elsa from *Frozen*. She would play with her princess dolls incessantly, sing the songs from the movie at the top of her lungs, and quote lines from memory as she played. She loved it. Her love—or obsession—stemmed from what she had seen and experienced from the movies and stories. However, she had never seen the real thing in person. She had never been to Disney World.

So you can imagine the sheer delight and euphoria when we announced at Christmas one year that we were going to Disney World. All the kids were thrilled to no end. They jumped up and down. They screamed. Little Harper kept saying, over and over, "Olaf is so silly . . . Olaf is so silly," referencing one of her other favorite characters from *Frozen*.

The day came, we arrived at Disney World, and it lived up to all the hype. Everything that my kids had heard about now was reality. It was no longer a story to them. It was tangible. It was one thing to hear stories, but a whole other thing to experience them in the flesh.

The same was true for the early followers of Jesus. By the time that John's Gospel was written, the predominant Greek philosophy of the day taught that all the deep questions in the world could be explained in something called the *Logos*. The philosophers Heraclitus and Aristotle actually used the *Logos* as a foundation in their philosophical works. It was the prevailing way of understanding the "higher power" that exists in life.

John, under the inspiration of God, used the opening stanzas of his account to shed more light on this *Logos*. He began by acknowledging the eternality of the *Logos* by saying it had existed since the beginning. In this way, he validated what his audience had understood for centuries. But John took it further by helping them understand that the *Logos* (Word) is connected to the *Theos* (God). In fact, the *Logos* (Word) is *Theos* (God). The *Logos* is more than a "higher power" or an "all-knowing" spirit. The *Logos* is God.

John was not finished providing clarity. He then took his readers into a deeper understanding of the *Logos* by explaining, "He was with God in the beginning . . . in him was life, and that life was the light of all mankind" (John 1:2, 4). In using the personal pronoun to identify the *Logos*, the Gospel writer was helping his readers understand that God was not some far-off being who was unable to identify with humanity. No, the *Logos* had definition and was knowable. The *Logos* had substance and was not a mysterious force.

John provided one more qualifier to help his readers understand the identity of the *Logos*: "The Word [*Logos*] became flesh and made his dwelling among us" (verse 14). The God of the universe, who up to this point resided in eternity, had broken out of his celestial home and taken up residence on earth. What was mystery was now reality. What was spirit was now flesh and blood. What had been experienced only by faith had now become sight.

What sets the Christian gospel apart from other belief systems is that "God . . . gave his one and only Son" for the world (John 3:16). Jesus, "being in very nature God, did not consider equality with God something to be used to his own advantage; rather, he made himself nothing by taking the very nature of a servant, being made in human likeness" (Philippians 2:6–7). God, in his grace, sent his Son to earth so that we could see him and believe in him.

In our Christian faith, we have more than just stories to go on. Jesus lived in a real time and real place. The Bible tells that he was born in Bethlehem, lived in Nazareth, worked in Galilee, and died and rose from the grave in Jerusalem. These are real places in the Near East Mediterranean region of the earth. Anyone alive today can visit these exact sites, walk the grounds, touch the dirt, and smell the aromas. *Seeing is believing.*

1. Have you ever visited a place after hearing about it for a long time? If so, how did your perspective change when you saw that place for the first time?

2. Why is it important that Jesus was a real person who existed at a real time in history and lived in a real place? What impact does that have on your faith?

READ

Waiting for a Messiah

The Jewish people in Jesus' day were waiting for God to send the promised Messiah. As far back as Genesis 3:15, when God issued a curse against humanity as a result of Adam and Eve's sin, he had announced a plan to send a Savior into the world: "I will put enmity between you [Satan] and the woman, and between your offspring and hers; he will crush your head, and you will strike his heel." God promised a child would be born who would crush the enemy.

The name of this child was not yet known, but it was clear that he would right the wrongs that Adam and Eve's sin had brought into the world. As the centuries passed, the prophet began to shed more light about this coming Messiah. Hundreds of years before the birth of Jesus, the prophet Isaiah foretold that a virgin would give birth to a son and he would be called Immanuel—God with Us. A couple of chapters later, the prophet provides these additional details about this coming Messiah:

> [6] *For to us a child is born,*
> *to us a son is given,*
> *and the government will be on his shoulders.*
> *And he will be called*
> *Wonderful Counselor, Mighty God,*
> *Everlasting Father, Prince of Peace.*
> [7] *Of the greatness of his government and peace*
> *there will be no end.*
> *He will reign on David's throne*
> *and over his kingdom,*
> *establishing and upholding it*
> *with justice and righteousness*
> *from that time on and forever.*
> *The zeal of the LORD Almighty*
> *will accomplish this.*

Isaiah 9:6–7

3. God promised to send a Savior immediately after Adam and Eve committed the first sin in the garden of Eden. What does this reveal about God?

4. What do the names Isaiah gives to the Messiah say about what his mission will be on the earth? What does Isaiah state about the nature of the Messiah's reign?

The Tension Builds

The final Old Testament prophet to testify about the coming of the Messiah was Malachi, who recorded these words from God: "I will send my messenger, who will prepare the way before me. Then suddenly the Lord you are seeking will come to his temple; the messenger of the covenant, whom you desire, will come" (Malachi 3:1). After this time, a period of 400 years of "silence" followed, where no further prophecies about the Messiah were made.

In those intervening years, a number of empires rose and fell. The people of Judah had previously been conquered by the Babylonians in 587 BC and taken into exile. The Persians had then become the dominant force in the region after defeating the Babylonians in 536 BC. Under their rule, the Jewish people were allowed to return to their homeland. A new power then arose in the form of a conqueror named Alexander the Great. He and his Macedonian army defeated the Persians in 336 BC, spreading Greek thought and philosophy (known as "Hellenism") throughout the territories that Persia possessed, including the land of Israel.

The death of Alexander in 323 BC led to his empire being divided into four "kingdoms" controlled by his generals, with the land of Israel falling under the rule of Ptolemy I Soter of Egypt. This kingdom lasted until it was defeated by the Syrians in 198 BC, at which time the land of Israel was annexed. In 165 BC, a man named Judas Maccabaeus led a revolt against the Syrians, retaking Jerusalem and ultimately winning Jewish independence in 142 BC. This independence lasted until 63 BC, when Pompey of Rome defeated the Syrians, entered Jerusalem, and took the land (now called Judea) as a possession of Rome.

All the while, the people of Israel were waiting in a state of prolonged tension for the promised Messiah to making his arrival on earth. The delay was causing caused much doubt and anxiety. But finally, the "messenger" of whom Malachi had prophesized appeared on the scene. The Gospel writers record the following about his birth and ministry in Judea:

> [11] *Then an angel of the Lord appeared to him, standing at the right side of the altar of incense.* [12] *When Zechariah saw him, he was startled and was gripped with fear.* [13] *But the angel said to him: "Do not be afraid, Zechariah; your prayer*

has been heard. Your wife Elizabeth will bear you a son, and you are to call him John. ¹⁴ He will be a joy and delight to you, and many will rejoice because of his birth, ¹⁵ for he will be great in the sight of the Lord. He is never to take wine or other fermented drink, and he will be filled with the Holy Spirit even before he is born. ¹⁶ He will bring back many of the people of Israel to the Lord their God. ¹⁷ And he will go on before the Lord, in the spirit and power of Elijah, to turn the hearts of the parents to their children and the disobedient to the wisdom of the righteous—to make ready a people prepared for the Lord."

Luke 1:11–17

¹ In those days John the Baptist came, preaching in the wilderness of Judea ² and saying, "Repent, for the kingdom of heaven has come near." ³ This is he who was spoken of through the prophet Isaiah:

> *"A voice of one calling in the wilderness,*
> *'Prepare the way for the Lord,*
> *make straight paths for him.'"*

⁴ John's clothes were made of camel's hair, and he had a leather belt around his waist. His food was locusts and wild honey. ⁵ People went out to him from Jerusalem and all Judea and the whole region of the Jordan. ⁶ Confessing their sins, they were baptized by him in the Jordan River.

Matthew 3:1–6

5. Why do you think God chose to be "silent" for 400 years and not send any prophet to announce the birth of Christ? What might he have been doing in that time of waiting?

6. How was John the Baptist a fulfillment of prophecies made in the Old Testament about the "messenger" who would precede the coming of the Messiah?

The Tension Is Resolved

John the Baptist was the one whom Isaiah had prophesied would be "a voice of one calling: 'In the wilderness prepare the way for the Lord; make straight in the desert a highway for our God" (Isaiah 40:3). Finally, the tension would be resolved. Matthew reveals how a woman named Mary, a virgin with child by the Holy Spirit, had a son who was Immanuel:

> ¹⁸ *This is how the birth of Jesus the Messiah came about: His mother Mary was pledged to be married to Joseph, but before they came together, she was found to be pregnant through the Holy Spirit.* ¹⁹ *Because Joseph her husband was faithful to the law, and yet did not want to expose her to public disgrace, he had in mind to divorce her quietly.*
>
> ²⁰ *But after he had considered this, an angel of the Lord appeared to him in a dream and said, "Joseph son of David, do not be afraid to take Mary home as your wife, because what is conceived in her is from the Holy Spirit.* ²¹ *She will give birth to a son, and you are to give him the name Jesus, because he will save his people from their sins."*
>
> ²² *All this took place to fulfill what the Lord had said through the prophet:* ²³ *"The virgin will conceive and give birth to a son, and they will call him Immanuel" (which means "God with us").*
>
> Matthew 1:18–23

John, a disciple of Jesus, picks up on this theme in his Gospel when he writes, "The Word [Jesus] became flesh and made his dwelling among us. We have seen his glory, the glory of the one and only Son, who came from the Father, full of grace and truth" (John 1:14). Jesus would dwell among the people in the New Testament just as the glory of God dwelt in the tabernacle and the temple in the Old Testament. Jesus was God—the glory of God and a man!

7. Joseph intended to divorce Mary when he discovered she was pregnant with a child who did not belong to him. What did the angel say to change his mind?

8. What does Jesus coming to earth in the flesh communicate about the nature of the gospel? How does the fact that he would choose to leave heaven bolster your faith?

REFLECT

It is fairly common for people to have overly simplistic or downright wrong views of Jesus. Some suggest that Jesus fits among the likes of the world's greatest teachers or moral exemplars. They claim that his life, and the record of his teachings, are meant to provide guidance for how we are meant to live. This is true to a degree, but it's woefully inadequate. Others believe that Jesus demonstrated how we should love others—especially the poor, marginalized, or outcast. Again, this is true, but it doesn't go far enough to capture the totality of why Jesus was sent.

Matthew tells us the mission. Mary is to give Immanuel the name Jesus, which captures the essence of his purpose. Jesus means *Savior*, and that is exactly what he will do: "He will save his people from their sins" (Matthew 1:21). This name, and its corresponding mission, should come as no surprise to those who are familiar with the story of the Bible.

As previously noted, back in Genesis 3:15, God had promised a Savior who would defeat Satan and sin. In Genesis 12:1–3, God promised his love to Abraham and his descendants, which is why Matthew traces the birth of Jesus through the line of Abraham (see Matthew 1:1). The various stories of the Old Testament reveal that the people were in need of such a Savior because they could never free themselves from sin. They returned to it again and again. Now, according to Matthew, the Savior of the world was here.

Jesus' birth should not have been surprising to the Jewish people, yet he came in a most unusual way for the One who would bring about God's salvation. Luke records that Mary and her husband, Joseph, were required to travel from Nazareth to Bethlehem to register for a census. While they were there, "The time came for the baby to be born, and she gave birth to her firstborn, a son. She wrapped him in cloths and placed him in a manger, because there was no guest room available for them" (Luke 2:6–7). Jesus' birth was not marked by the fanfare that one would expect for a Savior. Instead, his arrival was heralded by a few lowly shepherds (see verses 8–15).

We might be tempted to think of Jesus as a knee-jerk reaction from God. He had tried to save his people through Moses, the judges, David, the prophets, and others. They had all failed, and the people continued in their sinful rebellion, so now it was time for him to bring out the great once-for-all solution to the problem of sin. But the biblical authors don't present Jesus' birth as having come out of nowhere. They show him to be the promised answer all along.

For example, Matthew states the details of Jesus' coming were "to fulfill what the Lord had said through the prophet" (Matthew 1:22). Later, he describes the location of Jesus' birth as being "what the prophet has written" (2:5). Luke follows suit, stating that his intent in writing his Gospel is to show "the things that have been fulfilled among us" (Luke 1:1). Luke also writes about a devout man in Jerusalem who, on seeing the baby Jesus, quotes Old Testament prophecy: "A light for revelation to the Gentiles, and the glory of your people Israel" (2:32–34). The recurring echo of fulfilled prophecy shows that Jesus was God's plan all along.

Each of the figures in the Old Testament—Abraham, Moses, David, Isaiah, and others—pointed forward to Jesus' coming. Sadly, many missed Jesus because he wasn't the Savior they were expecting. The same is true in our day. People look for (or create) false saviors because they know they have a fundamental problem. Given a moment's reflection, all people know they don't live up to a standard—even a standard they have set for themselves. We all make mistakes. We all lie and deceive. We all fail to keep our word. We all squander God-given talent and potential. We all feel trapped in patterns of behavior that we know are harmful. While we might not define our actions as sin against a holy God, the reality is we know that we have fallen short of some standard and we need help. We want deliverance—salvation.

9. What are some of the wrong views you have heard people say about Jesus?

10. How do you think the Jewish people were expecting the Messiah to arrive?

CLOSE

We either find salvation through God's answer, Jesus Christ, or we invent a pseudo-savior. Some breathlessly pursue financial gain, thinking that wealth will deliver them and give them the life they are seeking. Some look to marriage or sex for an escape from whatever they consider to be a mundane life. But regardless of what people seek, it is important to note that all people look for a savior of some kind. We can't help it. In fact, if you look back over the story of your life, odds are you'll find several different "saviors" you have pursued through the years—relationships, possessions, success, comfort, and the like.

The fundamental dilemma with these types of saviors is that they always fall short. They over-promise and under-deliver. They ultimately collapse under the weight we place on them because no person or created thing can save. This was the predicament of the ancient Israelites who would consistently create idols made of silver, gold, or wood and worship them as gods. Repeatedly, God must remind people that idols are worthless to save because they are not God. The prophet Jeremiah didn't mince words when he wrote, "[Idols] are all senseless and foolish; they are taught by worthless wooden idols" (Jeremiah 10:8). Given enough time, we all say the same about the idols we worship in our day. They are worthless, impotent to save.

The failure of false saviors should awaken our appetite for God's Savior, Jesus Christ. Rather than looking for alternatives, we are to turn to God's eternal answer to the problem of human sin and brokenness in the world. Jesus is "the Savior of the world," which includes your life and your brokenness. He came to save you, so there's no need to look any further for the Savior you need. He's here and his name is Jesus.

11. What are some of the empty promises that pseudo-saviors make? How is Jesus helping you to overcome those false saviors and place your faith in him?

12. How does Jesus being the fulfillment of Old Testament prophecy give you confidence that he was who he said he was? Are there still any barriers to your belief in Jesus? If so, what are those barriers?

GOD-MAN

God said to Moses, "I AM WHO I AM. This is what you are to say to the Israelites: 'I AM has sent me to you.'"

EXODUS 3:14

For in Christ all the fullness of the Deity lives in bodily form, and in Christ you have been brought to fullness.

COLOSSIANS 2:9–10

When the set time
had fully come,
God sent his Son,
born of a woman.

GALATIANS 4:4

WELCOME

It is always comforting to have someone who "gets" you. A person who understands what you are going through in both the good times and the bad times. Someone who does not lecture you but instead is willing to just listen. They understand you and can relate with you.

I will never forget the season in my life right before my wife, Carmen, and I became engaged. I knew that I loved her, and I knew that I was going to ask her to marry me, but I was insecure and nervous. It was such a big decision! *Were we too young? Did we make enough money? Was I really ready to be a husband?* On and on the questions swirled in my mind.

In that season, I needed someone who had walked that road before to guide me. So I approached my dad. Now, you must understand, my dad and I have a great relationship. To this day, he is a very trusted confidant. However, at that time, we had never really talked about "love." I do not remember many conversations about marriage and dating. It may have been mentioned at surface level, but we certainly never got into exhaustive detail on the topic.

But to my surprise, when I approached my father about what I was thinking and feeling, he had great empathy for me. He walked me through the emotions that he had processed more than two decades before when he had asked my mom to marry him. He explained how he had navigated doubts about providing for a family, dealing with in-laws, and insecurities about whether she was "the one." We covered everything. No subject was off-limits.

It was a tremendous relief to have someone who had walked where I was about to walk to help me navigate the road ahead. I needed someone who could relate to my emotions in that season of my life. Likewise, some of the best comfort you will receive from others is when they let you know they have been where you currently are—that you are not alone in your experiences and you will get through your current ordeal.

When it comes to the gospel, there is good news. Jesus can relate to us in the seasons of life that we go through because he has walked through those seasons himself.

Our Savior can relate to both the joys and struggles we face. He is not a God who only knows about human weaknesses in theoretical terms. He knows about them in practical terms because he lived through them. As the writer of Hebrews says, "We do not have a high priest who is unable to empathize with our weaknesses, but we have one who has been tempted in every way, just as we are—yet he did not sin" (Hebrews 4:15). In Jesus, God came near to his people so that he could tangibly relate to them in a more intimate way.

1. Think of a time that you reached out someone who had "walked where you were walking" and provided guidance. What impact did that have on you?

2. When it comes to how you picture Jesus, do you see him as one who walked the road of life before and faced all that you face? How do you picture Jesus?

READ

Emotions on Display

Throughout the New Testament, we find many instances where Jesus displayed his humanity in his divinity. At the wedding feast at Cana, he performed his first miracle by turning water into really good wine (see John 2:10). However, in his humanity, Jesus was at this wedding as an invited guest (see verse 2). Given his mother's role as a concerned hostess when the wine ran out, it would seem this wedding was for friends of Jesus' family (see verse 3).

It is not hard to imagine Jesus having the same emotions that others have when attending a wedding—joy for the couple. He was excited for them. He relished in their happiness. He was glad they had found each other so they could share their lives together. Jesus identified with a celebratory human emotion. In the same way that we identify with the joy of others, Jesus also experience those same kind of emotions.

Jesus also knew how to mourn with those who were mourning. A few chapters later in the Gospel of John, we read of Jesus being informed that Lazarus, the brother of Mary and Martha, and one of his close friends, had fallen sick (see John 11:1-3). By the time Jesus arrived in the town of Bethany where the family lived, Lazarus had died. John relates what happened next:

> [17] *On his arrival, Jesus found that Lazarus had already been in the tomb for four days.* [18] *Now Bethany was less than two miles from Jerusalem,* [19] *and many Jews had come to Martha and Mary to comfort them in the loss of their brother.* [20] *When Martha heard that Jesus was coming, she went out to meet him, but Mary stayed at home. . . .*
>
> [28] *After she had said this, she went back and called her sister Mary aside. "The Teacher is here," she said, "and is asking for you."* [29] *When Mary heard this, she got up quickly and went to him.* [30] *Now Jesus had not yet entered the village, but was still at the place where Martha had met him.* [31] *When the Jews who had been with Mary in the house, comforting her, noticed how quickly she got up and went out, they followed her, supposing she was going to the tomb to mourn there.*
>
> [32] *When Mary reached the place where Jesus was and saw him, she fell at his feet and said, "Lord, if you had been here, my brother would not have died."*
>
> [33] *When Jesus saw her weeping, and the Jews who had come along with her also weeping, he was deeply moved in spirit and troubled.* [34] *"Where have you laid him?" he asked.*
>
> *"Come and see, Lord," they replied.*
>
> [35] *Jesus wept.*
>
> John 11:17–20, 28–35

Jesus was brokenhearted at the agony this caused his friends. He saw the pain they were enduring and wept with them. He did not rush to fix the problem—he would get to that later. Instead, he first met Mary and Martha where they were.

Several months ago, our church hosted a celebration of life for a young boy who had tragically died of a brain aneurism. The family had just started attending our church and did not have many personal relationships. But that did not stop the church from showing up. Many of our people showed up at the family home to comfort them. Others delivered meals. At the celebration, dozens of people came who did not know the family personally but wanted to be there to help them in their time of need.

Why? They identified with their pain. Many had been in their spot before and wanted help them through this very sad season.

Jesus is not a cosmic overlord who is unable to understand the plight of the human race. Quite the opposite—he can identify with humanity because knows our exact emotions. Seeing Jesus put his emotions on display helps us believe in his empathy for others too.

3. What does it say about Jesus that he was invited to celebrations like the wedding in Cana? What emotions do you envision him having toward the couple?

4. What does it say about Jesus that he was able to weep alongside his friends Mary and Martha? How do you picture Jesus interacting with them in the story?

Fully Human

Did you ever experience moving to a new city as a child? If so, then you know that with the move comes the challenge of making new friends in an unfamiliar school. There are few things more intimidating than walking into a classroom of middle schoolers as the new kid while everyone sizes you up. In the first few hours, most have formed an impression of who you are, what you are like, and whether or not they want to be your friend. We've all done it. Even if we haven't been the new kid, we've had our fair share of experiences with new kids and know how quickly we make up our minds about others. Certainly, we shouldn't "judge a book by its cover," but we do it all the time.

We can imagine how people attempted to size up Jesus in his early years. John records a bit of this reaction when Jesus began to gather the disciples who would join him in his mission. Philip told Nathanael, "We have found the one Moses wrote about in the Law, and about whom the prophets also wrote—Jesus of Nazareth, the son of Joseph." Nathanael's reply is telling: "Nazareth! Can anything good come from there?" (John 1:44–46).

Not only was Jesus maligned because of his hometown, but his unique upbringing was also called into question. After declaring himself to be the one sent from God to bring salvation, the Jewish leaders questioned, "Is this not Jesus, the son of Joseph, whose father and mother we know? How can he now say, 'I came down from heaven'?" (John 6:42). Nothing about Jesus would have indicated to most people that he was the Savior of the world.

The nature of Jesus' existence boggles the human mind. It is too rich for us to fully comprehend. Jesus was, at the same time, both fully God and fully man. He did not merely act like a person while remaining impervious to the plight actual people face. The author of Hebrews describes Jesus as one who was "tempted in every way, just as we are—yet he did not sin" (Hebrews 4:15). Matthew records an account of one such scene of temptation:

> [1] *Then Jesus was led by the Spirit into the wilderness to be tempted by the devil.*
> [2] *After fasting forty days and forty nights, he was hungry.* [3] *The tempter came to him and said, "If you are the Son of God, tell these stones to become bread."*

4 *Jesus answered, "It is written: 'Man shall not live on bread alone, but on every word that comes from the mouth of God.'"*

5 *Then the devil took him to the holy city and had him stand on the highest point of the temple.* 6 *"If you are the Son of God," he said, "throw yourself down. For it is written:*

> *"'He will command his angels concerning you,*
>   *and they will lift you up in their hands,*
>   *so that you will not strike your foot against a stone.'"*

7 *Jesus answered him, "It is also written: 'Do not put the Lord your God to the test.'"*

8 *Again, the devil took him to a very high mountain and showed him all the kingdoms of the world and their splendor.* 9 *"All this I will give you," he said, "if you will bow down and worship me."*

10 *Jesus said to him, "Away from me, Satan! For it is written: 'Worship the Lord your God, and serve him only.'"*

11 *Then the devil left him, and angels came and attended him.*

Matthew 4:1–11

It's easy for us to imagine Jesus as some Marvel comic book figure. We might think he was a superhero who merely gave the appearance of humanity but who in a moment could switch on his God-powers and do whatever he wanted. But as Paul writes, "He made himself nothing . . . being made in human likeness" (Philippians 2:7). Jesus willingly laid aside his divinity when he came to earth. He certainly possessed the power of God. As the mockers pointed out in his crucifixion, he could have called the angel armies to come and take him off the cross. But he didn't. He lived as a person, humbly submitting to the constraints of the human form.

This is what Paul has in mind when he says that Jesus laid aside equality with God (see verse 6). He had it all in heaven, yet he willingly gave of himself to become a human and enter a world that he all-too-well knew was broken by sin. Being all-knowing, Jesus fully understood the heinous sins that would be committed against him, ultimately leading to his death on a Roman cross. He willingly gave up his life, though he could have saved himself, as the ultimate act of humility and grace (see John 10:18). Jesus became human in all its grotesque realities.

5. In what ways was Jesus tempted as you are? Does it encourage you that Jesus is able to identify with you when you are tempted? Why or why not?

6. In what way did Jesus humble himself by becoming a man? To what extent was Jesus willing to humble himself?

Fully Divine

Jesus was not merely human, however. He was also fully God. Once again, we must be careful not to suggest that Jesus stopped being God when he came to this earth. He was no less the eternal one in whom, as John wrote in his Gospel, "all things were made" (John 1:3). He still possessed all power, glory, and fame even though he was now walking around in human form on earth. He was still the exalted one, the one above all others, and before whom all people will one day bow, acknowledging him as Lord (see Philippians 2:9–11).

The writer of Hebrews declares Jesus to be "the radiance of God's glory and the exact representation of his being" (Hebrews 1:3). He is the *exact* representation of God. Think of it this way. When artists create a portrait, they try to capture all the little details of their subject—hair color, facial features, skin tone, posture—to make their painting look as much like the real person as possible. But it is rare for artists to capture the *exact* representation of their subject . . . and friends and family who know the person well can point out the differences. The picture that artists create is never going to be an exact representation of reality.

Jesus was not a picture of God. He *is* God. Throughout his life, he demonstrated an ability to do things that only God could do, as the following passages reveal:

> 23 *Then he got into the boat and his disciples followed him.* 24 *Suddenly a furious storm came up on the lake, so that the waves swept over the boat. But Jesus was sleeping.* 25 *The disciples went and woke him, saying, "Lord, save us! We're going to drown!"*
>
> 26 *He replied, "You of little faith, why are you so afraid?" Then he got up and rebuked the winds and the waves, and it was completely calm.*
>
> 27 *The men were amazed and asked, "What kind of man is this? Even the winds and the waves obey him!"*
>
> Matthew 8:23–27

> 22 *Immediately Jesus made the disciples get into the boat and go on ahead of him to the other side, while he dismissed the crowd.* 23 *After he had dismissed them, he went up on a mountainside by himself to pray. Later that night, he was there alone,* 24 *and the boat was already a considerable distance from land, buffeted by the waves because the wind was against it.*
>
> 25 *Shortly before dawn Jesus went out to them, walking on the lake.* 26 *When the disciples saw him walking on the lake, they were terrified. "It's a ghost," they said, and cried out in fear.*
>
> 27 *But Jesus immediately said to them: "Take courage! It is I. Don't be afraid."*
>
> 28 *"Lord, if it's you," Peter replied, "tell me to come to you on the water."*
>
> 29 *"Come," he said.*
>
> *Then Peter got down out of the boat, walked on the water and came toward Jesus.* 30 *But when he saw the wind, he was afraid and, beginning to sink, cried out, "Lord, save me!"*
>
> 31 *Immediately Jesus reached out his hand and caught him. "You of little faith," he said, "why did you doubt?"*
>
> 32 *And when they climbed into the boat, the wind died down.* 33 *Then those who were in the boat worshiped him, saying, "Truly you are the Son of God."*
>
> Matthew 14:22–33

In John's Gospel, Jesus used a striking phrase to speak about himself, declaring that before Abraham was, "I am" (John 8:58). Not only did Jesus point out that he existed before Abraham—a claim that would have been stunning in itself—but he also used a phrase that God had spoken to Moses long ago. Moses, fearful of the task he had been given, had said to God, "Suppose I go to the Israelites and say to them, 'The God of your fathers has sent me to you,' and they ask me, 'What is his name?' Then what shall I tell them?" (Exodus 3:13).

Moses wanted God to put his name on the line as the one who was making this bold request, but he didn't even know God's name. The Lord replied to him, "'I AM WHO I AM.' This is what you are to say to the Israelites: 'I AM has sent me to you'" (verse 14). God revealed that his name was "I AM," indicating that he is the God who has always been, who is, and who will always be. That was all Moses and the Israelites needed to know.

Thousands of years later, Jesus applied this name to himself. God, the great I AM, was Jesus, and Jesus was God. It is this claim, more than any other, that leads to Jesus' execution. The Jewish leaders could deal with another great teacher. They could even cope with someone who performed miracles. But they could not tolerate someone who claimed to be God. We see this in Luke's Gospel, where the Jewish leaders asked Jesus directly whether he was the Son of the God, and Jesus replied, "It is as you say" (Luke 22:70 NKJV). In the very next verse, the Jewish leaders say that Jesus must be killed for blasphemy because he claimed to be God.

7.   How do the stories of Jesus calming the storms reveal he was fully God? How did the disciples react in both stories when they witnessed Jesus' divine power?

8. Why is it so important that Jesus was both fully man *and* fully God? (Think of what would happen if you took one of these away. What would happen, for example, if Jesus were not fully man? Conversely, what would happen if he were not fully God?)

REFLECT

There are few additional points to consider as it relates to Jesus being fully both fully God and fully human. First, if Jesus were not fully man, as we have already seen, this would certainly negate or minimize his ability to care for us as a faithful priest and father, because he would not know fully what it was like to be tempted in a broken world.

As humans, we have incurred a great penalty for our sin. We have all broken God's law and are rightly deserving of death. The Old Testament allowed for the blood of bulls and goats to satisfy the price for human sin, but it was impossible for the blood of animals to pay the price for human sin. The payment for sin must therefore be paid by a human—a human sacrifice. Jesus, being fully human, was capable of substituting himself for the sins of fellow people.

Second, if Jesus were not fully God, he would lack the power and authority to be our Savior. In being fully God, Jesus was able to be a perfect substitute. If Jesus were a mere mortal, stained and marred by sin, his sacrifice would have no merit, because he would have to offer a sacrifice for himself as well, just like the priests of the Old

Testament had to do. But Jesus was perfect. There was no stain of sin in his life. He never sinned—not in what he thought, what he did, or what he did not do. He was perfect, which meant that he could offer his life as a perfect sacrifice and know that God would accept this payment once and for all.

As you reflect on this week's lesson, consider the miracle that is Jesus being fully God and fully man. This reality is what has set Jesus apart from all who claim some type of godlike status. There is real power in who Jesus is because of his status as the God-man. No other supposed god is like Jesus.

9. What would Jesus *not* have been able to do for us if he were not fully human? What would he *not* have been able to do for us if he were not also fully divine?

10. As you reflect on Jesus being the God-man, what are the biggest barriers that you have to overcome in your own mind? Why those particular barriers?

CLOSE

The beauty of God's plan is mind-boggling. It's certainly not a plan that any of us could have created. There are many throughout history who have supposedly demonstrated God's wisdom and instructed humankind on how they should live. There are those who have performed great deeds of love, mercy, and compassion. But there is only one God who did what Jesus did. There is only one God-man, Jesus Christ, who was the great fulfillment of God's eternal plan and the one capable of bringing salvation to a sin-ravished world.

11. Think of a struggle or challenge that you are facing right now in your life. How do you think Jesus feels about what you are facing? How do you see him identifying with you?

12. In what ways does Jesus' ability to empathize with you give you hope?

Lesson Three

MISSION

*But Moses sought the favor of the L*ᴏʀᴅ *his God.*
*"L*ᴏʀᴅ*," he said, "why should your anger burn against your*
people, whom you brought out of Egypt with great
power and a mighty hand?"

EXODUS 32:11

For this reason Christ is the mediator of a new covenant,
that those who are called may receive the promised
eternal inheritance—now that he has died as a ransom to
set them free from the sins committed under the
first covenant.

HEBREWS 9:15

Whatever you do,

do it all

for the glory

of God.

1 CORINTHIANS 10:31

WELCOME

Carmen and I lived in New York City as church planters for most of the 2000s. When we first arrived we were filled with hope. Our primary focus was reaching out to university-aged students, sharing the gospel, and then—God willing—starting a new church on their campus.

But in those early days in the city, we were overwhelmed. There were about one million students within the metro area of New York City at the time, and the thought of making even a little dent in the need was inconceivable. We were just two people, wide-eyed and full of faith.

Carmen and I had attended a Passion Conference and knew of its influence among college students. I felt like Passion could be helpful to us, so, somewhat naively, I reached out and asked if they would come and help. To my great encouragement, they responded yes.

We ended up planning a city-wide worship night together. But the challenge was that at this time, no one did these kinds of "big" Christian events in New York for college students. The cost was too high, and the interest was too low. Nevertheless, we stepped out in faith and rented the largest Broadway-style theater that we could find—the Beacon on the Upper West Side. We worked hard to get the word out and prayed a lot.

To make a long story short, we were completely blown away by all that God did. The nearly 3,000-seat theater was jammed full of students worshipping Jesus. It was incredible! The most enduring memory of the night was the sight of about a dozen students from one of the military academies, in their uniforms, just going for it in worship. More than twenty years later, I still have a photograph of them hanging in my office today.

For me, that night served as a reminder that God is going to be glorified. Even in a place like New York City where the conventional wisdom says that no one really cares about God, he will make his name known. He is, after all, on a mission. A mission for . . . God.

This statement might catch you off guard. Perhaps you have been taught that God is on a mission for people. Or maybe you learned that God is on a mission for the church. You would not be wrong in either assertion. However, the reason that God is on a mission for people and for his church is because he is on a mission for God.

Biblical scholars refer to this concept as the *Missio Dei*, a Latin term that dates as far back as the fourth century AD and simply means "mission of God." The *Missio Dei* is ultimately about the people in the church partnering with God to magnify him and bring glory to his name. It is a mission to help all of humankind recognize that God has created us as a reflection of himself and that there is nothing that we can do apart from him.

The idea that God is on a mission for God is consistent with his character. If he is ultimate in the universe—supreme and all powerful—then his mission cannot be focused on anything else. If it were, it would serve to diminish who he is.

1. When is a time that you saw God do something miraculous for his glory?

2. Why does God's goal in his mission have to be focused on his own glory?

READ

The Ultimate Aim of God

Throughout the Old Testament, we find that the ultimate aim of God is to bring glory to himself. In Psalm 8:1, David writes, "Lord, our Lord, how majestic is your name in all the earth! You have set your glory in the heavens." In Psalm 19:1, he states, "The heavens declare the glory of God." Isaiah also wrote of a vision he received in which angelic beings proclaimed to one another, "Holy, holy, holy is the Lord Almighty; the whole earth is full of his glory" (Isaiah 6:3).

God is after his own glory. This is not because he is an egomaniac (in the way we understand the term) but because he knows that our ultimate satisfaction will only be found when we, as humans, rest in his sufficiency and supremacy. Sadly, the people of God have often gotten this wrong. Back in Genesis 11, we find one such instance where the people departed from their long-term understanding of who God was and started bringing glory to themselves—relying on their own abilities instead of their faith in the Lord. The culmination of this self-glorification was building a tower to the heavens, as the following passage relates:

> ¹ *Now the whole world had one language and a common speech.* ² *As people moved eastward, they found a plain in Shinar and settled there.*
>
> ³ *They said to each other, "Come, let's make bricks and bake them thoroughly." They used brick instead of stone, and tar for mortar.* ⁴ *Then they said,*

"Come, let us build ourselves a city, with a tower that reaches to the heavens, so that we may make a name for ourselves; otherwise we will be scattered over the face of the whole earth."

5 But the LORD came down to see the city and the tower the people were building. 6 The LORD said, "If as one people speaking the same language they have begun to do this, then nothing they plan to do will be impossible for them. 7 Come, let us go down and confuse their language so they will not understand each other."

8 So the LORD scattered them from there over all the earth, and they stopped building the city. 9 That is why it was called Babel—because there the LORD confused the language of the whole world. From there the LORD scattered them over the face of the whole earth.

Genesis 11:1–9

Notice the people's reason for building the tower, which reveals the heart behind their actions: "Come, let us build ourselves a city, with a tower that reaches to the heavens, so that we may make a name for ourselves" (verse 4). The Lord's response to their actions was to confuse their language and scatter them across the earth. Shortly after, we read of God calling Abram to reestablish his mission of bringing glory to himself on earth (see Genesis 12:1–3).

The Westminster Shorter Catechism states that "the chief end of man is to glorify God and enjoy him forever." This profound purpose encapsulates the essence of human existence, providing our direction in life and our source of fulfillment. "To glorify God" implies recognizing the divine as the ultimate foundation of meaning and goodness in our lives, acknowledging our dependence on him for guidance and sustenance. This recognition fosters humility, gratitude, and a sense of purpose within us that transcends the mundane.

"Enjoying God" is not a passive pursuit but an active engagement with him. It means finding joy in the beauty of creation, the complexity of human relationships, and the pursuit of knowledge, all of which are manifestations of God's wisdom and love. This enjoyment leads to a sense of wonder, gratitude, and contentment that permeates every aspect of our lives.

Ultimately, the dual purpose of glorifying and enjoying God creates a harmonious cycle. As we glorify God by living according to his principles of love, compassion, and justice, we are immersed in an abiding joy that springs from living a life of purpose and integrity. In turn, this joy fuels our desire to continue glorifying and enjoying God, creating a spiritual equilibrium that enriches our existence and empowers us to make a positive impact on the world.

3. What were the builders of the Tower of Babel attempting to accomplish through their own efforts? Why did God decide to cut this mission short?

4. What does "glorifying God" and "enjoying God" look like in your life?

Jesus' Mission on Earth

As we turn to the New Testament, we find that Jesus' mission was also to glorify the Father. Hebrews 1:3 tells us that "the Son is the radiance of God's glory and the exact representation of his being, sustaining all things by his powerful word." Yes, the mission of Jesus is about people. Yes, his desire is for people to come to faith. Yes, he desires that people will spend eternity in heaven with him. But his ultimate aim is to glorify God the Father. In the following passage, the apostle Paul gives us a more complete picture of Jesus' mission on earth:

> [9] *Therefore God exalted him to the highest place*
> *and gave him the name that is above every name,*
> [10] *that at the name of Jesus every knee should bow,*
> *in heaven and on earth and under the earth,*
> [11] *and every tongue acknowledge that Jesus Christ is Lord,*
> *to the glory of God the Father.*

Philippians 2:9–11

Paul reveals that Jesus' mission of salvation is ultimately about the glory of God. People are sinful and do not reflect God's glory. Since the time that Adam and Eve rebelled against God in the garden of Eden, all people have been estranged from God because of their sin. Paul uses harsh language in the book of Romans to speak of this reality. He writes that "all have sinned and fall short of the glory of God" (3:23). We became "God's enemies" because of our sinful identity and actions (5:10). God did not turn his back on us. We all have turned our backs on him and chosen, instead, to live gratifying our sinful desires. We became his enemies.

What are the consequences? Paul states, "the wages of sin is death" (6:23). However, there is good news for us, for Paul continues, "but the gift of God is eternal life in Christ Jesus our Lord." God made a way, through Jesus, for us to be reconciled to himself. He rescued us from the wages of our sin by dying in our place. Paul makes this point when he writes, "God demonstrates his own love for us in this: While we were still sinners, Christ died for us" (5:8).

Notice the emphasis here. God did not wait for his enemies—which included us—to change their ways before he saved them. Rather, he saved them *while* they were sinners, *while* they were his enemies, *while* they mocked his love, and *while* they turned their back on him. God saved his enemies while they were still his enemies—and he did so by dying for them! This is a far better and more beautiful story than anything Hollywood could create.

5. How does Jesus' mission of bringing salvation to humanity connect with God's ultimate goal of bringing glory to himself? How are the two related?

6. How do you react to the fact that your sin makes you an enemy of God? How have you seen God extend his love to you while you were still his enemy?

God Saves His Enemies

Jesus understood his mission in light of God's mission to bring glory to himself by offering salvation to his enemies. From the earliest stages of Jesus' work on earth, he was notorious for hanging out with those on the margins of societies. You know the kind—the ones marked by society as rebellious, wicked, or foolish. Those were the kind of people Jesus pursued, and he did this so regularly that he built a bit of a reputation for being a "friend" of sinners.

The religious leaders of Jesus' day found it hard to understand how the One who claimed to be God's promised Savior could love people like this. Mark records Jesus' response to one such accusation: "It is not the healthy who need a doctor, but the sick. I have not come to call the righteous, but sinners" (2:17). Jesus' mission was to provide a way for sinful people, who do not reflect God's glory, to be reconciled with their heavenly Father. Other accounts in the Gospels highlight this reality, such as the following story:

¹ *Now Jesus learned that the Pharisees had heard that he was gaining and baptizing more disciples than John—* ² *although in fact it was not Jesus who baptized, but his disciples.* ³ *So he left Judea and went back once more to Galilee.*

⁴ *Now he had to go through Samaria.* ⁵ *So he came to a town in Samaria called Sychar, near the plot of ground Jacob had given to his son Joseph.* ⁶ *Jacob's well was there, and Jesus, tired as he was from the journey, sat down by the well. It was about noon.*

⁷ *When a Samaritan woman came to draw water, Jesus said to her, "Will you give me a drink?"* ⁸ *(His disciples had gone into the town to buy food.)*

⁹ *The Samaritan woman said to him, "You are a Jew and I am a Samaritan woman. How can you ask me for a drink?" (For Jews do not associate with Samaritans.)*

¹⁰ *Jesus answered her, "If you knew the gift of God and who it is that asks you for a drink, you would have asked him and he would have given you living water."*

¹¹ *"Sir," the woman said, "you have nothing to draw with and the well is deep. Where can you get this living water?* ¹² *Are you greater than our father Jacob, who gave us the well and drank from it himself, as did also his sons and his livestock?"*

¹³ *Jesus answered, "Everyone who drinks this water will be thirsty again,* ¹⁴ *but whoever drinks the water I give them will never thirst. Indeed, the water I give them will become in them a spring of water welling up to eternal life."*

¹⁵ *The woman said to him, "Sir, give me this water so that I won't get thirsty and have to keep coming here to draw water."*

¹⁶ *He told her, "Go, call your husband and come back."*

¹⁷ *"I have no husband," she replied.*

Jesus said to her, "You are right when you say you have no husband. ¹⁸ *The fact is, you have had five husbands, and the man you now have is not your husband. What you have just said is quite true."*

¹⁹ *"Sir," the woman said, "I can see that you are a prophet.* ²⁰ *Our ancestors worshiped on this mountain, but you Jews claim that the place where we must worship is in Jerusalem."*

²¹ *"Woman," Jesus replied, "believe me, a time is coming when you will worship the Father neither on this mountain nor in Jerusalem.* ²² *You*

Samaritans worship what you do not know; we worship what we do know, for salvation is from the Jews. 23 Yet a time is coming and has now come when the true worshipers will worship the Father in the Spirit and in truth, for they are the kind of worshipers the Father seeks. 24 God is spirit, and his worshipers must worship in the Spirit and in truth."

25 The woman said, "I know that Messiah" (called Christ) "is coming. When he comes, he will explain everything to us."

26 Then Jesus declared, "I, the one speaking to you—I am he."

John 4:1–26

It would be hard to imagine a more unlikely interaction based on the cultural norms of Jesus' day. First, she was a woman, which would have made this encounter with a male Jewish teacher highly unusual. Second, she was a Samaritan, a people group that resulted from the mixed marriages between Jews and Gentiles. They were thought to be inferior people and were avoided by "good" Jews of the day. To cap it off, she had a reputation. Not only did she have a past, but she also had a present. She was one of "those" people.

Jesus knew all this. He was not blind to the reality of her situation. He even knew the sinful pockets of her life that she was trying to hide. He was fully aware of just how messed up she was. Still, Jesus extended love to this woman. It sounds simple, but consider the magnitude of this truth. The eternal, perfect Son of God loved a sinner like this enough to offer her salvation. We know that at the end of their conversation she believed because, shortly after, John writes, "Many of the Samaritans from that town believed in him because of the woman's testimony" (John 4:39). Not only did God save her, but he also saved others through her.

This type of story gets repeated again and again. In Luke 8:26–39, Jesus saves a demoniac. This was a bad dude. He lived in a graveyard, naked, with no home. People tried to bind him with chains to keep him under control, but he would break the chains and go berserk. You would imagine the entire town was mortified by their demon-possessed resident. Surely, the Son of God would want nothing to do with a guy like this. There were good people in the city, those who did what was right and lived upstanding lives. Jesus would have every reason to love people like them, but not a demon-possessed man living in the tombs.

But that is just what Jesus did. He went to the man, cast out his demons, and saved him. Just like the Samaritan woman, he then sent the man back into the town to tell others how much the Savior had done for him (see verse 39). It would have been great to watch those conversations as the once-demon-possessed man walked back into town and shared the story with those who had given up on him. We are told that those who saw him sitting at Jesus' feet in his right mind were afraid (see verse 35). They likely couldn't even grasp that type of change.

Jesus saves sinners. It's the theme of his life. Outcasts, rebels, known deceivers, the sexually immoral, those marked by disease, those written off by society—Jesus extended the love of God and offer of salvation to all. In the process, he proved that God saves his enemies, even while they are still bent on rebelling against him.

7.   What do you observe about Jesus' mission based on the story of the Samaritan woman? Why was she an "unlikely target" of God's love based on the norms of the day?

8.   What does Jesus' mission of reaching out to people like the Samaritan woman and demon-possessed say about the types of people we should be reaching in our mission?

REFLECT

There are several different ways the theme of this lesson might be landing with you. Maybe today you feel that you are undeserving of God's love. You know you have made a mess of this life. Others have written you off. You have been labeled and discarded by those who were supposed to care about you. You have been told—whether directly or through people's actions—that you are unlovable. You've heard of the love of God, but your immediate thought is, *That's nice for some people, but I'm too far gone. God can't love someone like me.*

If this is your story, know that you are just the kind of person that Jesus came to save. A God who loves and saves an adulterous woman, a demon-possessed man, and countless other known sinners can surely save you. In fact, he came into this world for people like you. Regardless of your past or present, you can call out to him right now and experience his love.

Or perhaps, as you consider this week's study, you fear that your story is somehow too normal. You don't have a notorious past—at least not the kind that makes for the radical conversion stories you have heard from others. Maybe you heard the gospel as a child, professed faith at an early age, and avoided many of the sins that have plagued others of your age.

If this is you, know that God's truth for you is the same. You were once an enemy of God, regardless of how good you think your life has been when compared to others. You may have demonstrated that reality differently than others—perhaps through pride or self-sufficiency rather than sexual immorality or addiction. We were all born into this world as God's enemies . . . sinners by nature and choice. So even if your story doesn't feel as radical, realize that you were no more deserving of God's love than anyone else. At the same time, if you have been saved by Jesus, you have no need to feel insecure about your past. You don't need to feel inadequate when you compare your story to the salvation journey of others. Anyone who has been saved, regardless of his or her story, is a trophy of God's love and grace.

Finally, you might be among the group who is unwilling to admit just how messed up you actually are. In this case, know that pride is the enemy of salvation. It will keep you from owning your sin and humbling yourself in repentance and faith. You only have to look at how Jesus interacted with the religious leaders of his day—who thought they had their act together, obeyed God's law, and were not like the "other" sinners—to understand the consequences. They were too proud to recognize their need to accept Jesus' offer of salvation. Jesus said of them, "How will you escape being condemned to hell?" (Matthew 23:33).

9. In which of these three groups do you find yourself today? What do you sense God is saying to you today as it relates to his offer of love and salvation?

10. Why is pride such an obstacle to experiencing the love of God? What steps do you need to take today to renounce any pride that has crept into your life?

CLOSE

Jesus' warning to the religious leaders of his day should serve as a warning to us in our day. We are on dangerous ground if we refuse to believe that God would ever consider us his enemies. As James wrote, "God opposes the proud but shows favor to the humble" (4:6). We might take pride in the fact we're pretty good people—that we try to do what is right, love others, and care for the world. And, by all human standards, we are better than most.

The problem with this type of thinking is that God doesn't measure whether we have missed the mark or not by human standards. He measures us according to his standard of holiness. Paul wrote, "All who sin under the law will be judged by the law" (Romans 2:12). This means that anyone who has ever committed a sin according to God's standard of holiness is guilty of violating his law and thus subject to its penalty—which is death. Paul continued, "There is no one righteous . . . therefore no one will be declared righteous in God's sight by the works of the law" (3:10, 20). This means that every person is guilty of missing God's mark.

We need to heed Jesus' word that he came "to seek and to save the lost" (Luke 19:10). Only those who admit they are lost can be found. Those who are unwilling to admit their sin will miss the love of God, even though they think they have it all along.

11. What are some steps you can begin to take to better align yourself with the mission of God?

12. What are the biggest barriers you will face in aligning with his mission? How can the people in your church community help you overcome those barriers?

Lesson Four

KINGDOM

Yours, Lord, is the greatness and the power and the glory and the majesty and the splendor, for everything in heaven and earth is yours. Yours, Lord, is the kingdom; you are exalted as head over all.

1 CHRONICLES 29:11

"But seek first his kingdom and his righteousness, and all these things will be given to you as well."

MATTHEW 6:33

"The greatest
among you
will be
your servant."

MATTHEW 23:11

WELCOME

In my younger days, basketball was more than just a sport to me. It was a passion and a calling. I played basketball throughout high school and into my early years of college. During those years, I developed a strong sense of pride in my abilities on the court.

One semester in college, I found myself facing a requirement to take a basketball class for a physical education credit. I walked into the class with an air of confidence, convinced that it would be a breeze. After all, the class was filled with everyday college students, many of whom had never played basketball before. They were there merely to earn an easy PE credit. I, on the other hand, thought this class was beneath me, from a basketball standpoint.

The class was led by the assistant basketball coach at our university. As the semester wore on, we practiced dribbling, shooting, and the basics of the game. But it was toward the end of the semester that the real challenge emerged. The coach decided to organize a three-on-three tournament, and he handpicked the teams. He paired me up with a fairly skilled player and another student named Dan. Dan was a foreign exchange student from China, barely five feet tall, and appeared to have little to no experience with basketball.

When the tournament began, our team breezed through the first couple of rounds. But as the competition got tougher, we started to struggle and the losses began to pile up. My frustration was mounting. In the heat of the game, I began to yell at Dan for not playing up to my standards. I desperately wanted to win, but my behavior was far from admirable.

The coach, who had been observing the game, called a timeout. He directed me to the bench and took the court himself, joining Dan and my other teammate. He became a player-coach, orchestrating the game like a maestro. He used hand signals to indicate where they should stand, when to set screens, and where to make cuts. The three of them moved on the court like a well-coordinated team, executing plays they had never practiced before.

As the game neared its end, the coach set Dan up for an easy bucket. He signaled to Dan where to run, passed him the ball . . . and Dan scored. My team won the game. I sat on the sideline the entire time, humbled as I reflected on my behavior.

This humbling experience was a turning point for me. The coach's actions spoke volumes about leadership, teamwork, and the importance of treating others with respect, regardless of their skill level. I learned that true leadership involved lifting others up, not tearing them down. It was a lesson I would carry with me far beyond the basketball court. The most significant victories in life come not from individual prowess but from working together as a team, treating others with kindness, valuing their contributions, and seeking to serve them rather than being served.

Jesus said these are the same traits that lead to greatness in God's kingdom. The opening verse of the Bible proclaims, "In the beginning God created the heavens and the earth" (Genesis 1:1). God is the creator of all, and "everything in heaven and earth" belongs to him as he is "exalted as head over all" (1 Chronicles 29:11). God has established his rule over this earth as a king rules over a kingdom. David establishes this truth when he writes, "The Lord has established his throne in heaven, and his kingdom rules over all" (Psalm 103:19).

We know from history that earthly kings do not willingly give up their power. They hold on to it with everything they have, often oppressing their subjects in the process. Earthly kingdoms teach us that greatness is found in strength and domination. But Jesus revealed that God's kingdom is completely different and upside-down from this way of thinking. In the kingdom of God, the most powerful are not those who serve but those who serve others.

Jesus, though divine, did not wield his power over humanity. In fact, he did the exact opposite. He became a servant to humanity first by becoming a human, and then he "humbled himself by becoming obedient to death—even death on a cross!"

(Philippians 2:8). Jesus taught that those who are great in God's kingdom are not those whom the world considers to be great. Rather, he said, "Blessed are the poor in spirit, for theirs is the kingdom of heaven. . . . Blessed are the meek, for they will inherit the earth. . . . Blessed are those who are persecuted because of righteousness, for theirs is the kingdom of heaven" (Matthew 5:3, 5, 10).

Later in that same chapter in Matthew's Gospel, Jesus tells his followers, "If anyone slaps you on the right cheek, turn to them the other cheek also" (verse 39), and, "Love your enemies and pray for those who persecute you" (verse 44). On the surface, these ideas sound radical. When someone attacks us, our natural human response is to strike back against them. But it is not really radical when we understand another principle that Jesus taught: "Greater love has no one than this: to lay down one's life for one's friends" (John 15:13).

Jesus demonstrated that if a person is willing to lose his or her life for others, that person is willing to do anything for them. "Jesus Christ laid down his life for us. And we ought to lay down our lives for our brothers and sisters" (1 John 3:16). Seeing Jesus live out the upside-down nature of God's kingdom makes us believe that radically serving others is possible.

1. When is a time that you achieved success by working with others on a team and valuing their contributions instead of going it alone?

2. How do you respond to the fact that Jesus calls all members of God's kingdom to love and serve others? How easy or difficult do you find that to do?

READ

Jesus Announces God's Kingdom

What are some of your most memorable days? One of mine is my wedding day. Even though Carmen and I have been married for more than twenty-five years, I remember it like it was yesterday. I recall the sights and sounds and the people who were there. I also vividly remember my first basketball game in high school, when I was named to the starting lineup. I can still picture the team we were playing, the number of points that I scored, and the reaction of the fans. I remember the emotion that my dad had. It was an epic day!

Not all days are equal. Most simply involve moving from one task to another. Other days are fraught with chaos, due to something unexpected like a sickness or accident. Periodically, you will have a great day where you accomplish something significant at work, establish new relationships, or celebrate a milestone. At the end of a given year, you are unlikely to remember the normal days. But the unexpected and unpredictable days—the ones involving graduations, job promotions, marriages, childbirths, and the like—will stick with you. Over the course of your life, it will be the unique days that will define your identity, give shape to your life, and make your story unique from other people's stories.

The authors of the New Testament, particularly those who wrote the Gospels, made no attempt to record every detail of Jesus' life. Luke, the author of both the Gospel bearing his name and the book of Acts, introduces his letter saying he carefully investigated the claims regarding Jesus Christ and constructed an orderly account of the details (see Luke 1:1–4). These details do not recount everything Jesus did or said. In fact, there is almost nothing written about the first three decades of Jesus' life. Instead, we are given highlights of Jesus' work over three key years in his earthly ministry, leading up to his death, burial, and resurrection.

When John the Baptist appeared to prepare the way for the Messiah, he told the crowds, "Repent, for the kingdom of heaven has come near" (Matthew 3:2). Shortly after, Jesus inaugurated his ministry in the synagogue of his hometown in Nazareth. As the following passage relates, Jesus told his fellow Nazarenes what this kingdom would look like:

⁶ *He went to Nazareth, where he had been brought up, and on the Sabbath day he went into the synagogue, as was his custom. He stood up to read,* ¹⁷ *and the scroll of the prophet Isaiah was handed to him. Unrolling it, he found the place where it is written:*

> ¹⁸ *"The Spirit of the Lord is on me,*
> *because he has anointed me*
> *to proclaim good news to the poor.*
> *He has sent me to proclaim freedom for the prisoners*
> *and recovery of sight for the blind,*
> *to set the oppressed free,*
> ¹⁹ *to proclaim the year of the Lord's favor."*

²⁰ *Then he rolled up the scroll, gave it back to the attendant and sat down. The eyes of everyone in the synagogue were fastened on him.* ²¹ *He began by saying to them, "Today this scripture is fulfilled in your hearing."*

Luke 4:16–21

"The kingdom of heaven" was at the forefront of Jesus' mind as he spoke these words, and he talked about it frequently throughout his ministry. The word *kingdom*, of course, conjures up images of a king. Jesus, the King of kings, was bringing God's kingdom to this earth. He even taught his disciples to pray that God's kingdom would come on earth as it was in heaven (see Matthew 6:10). The kingdom of God thus represents how things are in heaven, where peace, beauty, joy, rest, and worship are always on display. It is the way God intended the world to function—a paradise like the garden of Eden free of sin and suffering.

3. When you hear the phrase "the kingdom of God," what ideas or images come to mind?

4. Based on Jesus' words in Luke 4:18–19, what is the kingdom of God like?

Jesus Teaches About God's Kingdom

Jesus came to bring the kingdom of God to earth. He did this in two primary ways: (1) he taught about the kingdom, and (2) he demonstrated the kingdom. It's kind of like show-and-tell back in elementary school—those days when students would walk into class with some poor praying mantis in a mason jar with two holes punched in the top. They would traumatize the bug by rattling the jar and then announce to the class all the interesting and disgusting things they had learned about their newfound praying mantis friend. Those were the days!

Show-and-tell works when there is something interesting and unusual to talk about— an animal people haven't seen up close, a place they have never been, a concept they have read about but don't understand, a culture that is foreign to them. Show-and-tell takes unfamiliar things and makes them more understandable and relatable for people. This is just what Jesus does when he teaches about God's kingdom. Certainly, there nothing less familiar to sinful humans than the kingdom of God. We know darkness, pain, and brokenness, but it is hard for us to imagine heaven. So, Jesus comes down to our level and does a little show-and-tell.

The Bible reveals that Jesus taught the people of his day using parables. These were simple, relevant stories that Jesus used to illustrate deeper spiritual truths about God and his kingdom. Jesus drew on imagery in these stories that was familiar to his listeners—seeds, yeast, pearls, nets, fish, and the like. In the following passages, we see Jesus telling a series of these short parables to communicate what the king-dom of God was like:

> [31] *He told them another parable: "The kingdom of heaven is like a mustard seed, which a man took and planted in his field.* [32] *Though it is the smallest of*

all seeds, yet when it grows, it is the largest of garden plants and becomes a tree, so that the birds come and perch in its branches."

³³ He told them still another parable: "The kingdom of heaven is like yeast that a woman took and mixed into about sixty pounds of flour until it worked all through the dough."

³⁴ Jesus spoke all these things to the crowd in parables; he did not say anything to them without using a parable.

Matthew 13:31-34

⁴⁴ "The kingdom of heaven is like treasure hidden in a field. When a man found it, he hid it again, and then in his joy went and sold all he had and bought that field.

⁴⁵ "Again, the kingdom of heaven is like a merchant looking for fine pearls. ⁴⁶ When he found one of great value, he went away and sold everything he had and bought it.

⁴⁷ "Once again, the kingdom of heaven is like a net that was let down into the lake and caught all kinds of fish. ⁴⁸ When it was full, the fishermen pulled it up on the shore. Then they sat down and collected the good fish in baskets, but threw the bad away. ⁴⁹ This is how it will be at the end of the age. The angels will come and separate the wicked from the righteous ⁵⁰ and throw them into the blazing furnace, where there will be weeping and gnashing of teeth.

Matthew 13:44-50

5. What do the parables in Matthew 13:31–34 reveal about the nature of God's kingdom? What was Jesus saying about the power of God's kingdom to change people's lives?

6. What do the parables in Matthew 13:44–46 reveal about the importance that God's kingdom should have in our lives? In the parable of the nets found in Matthew 13:47–50, what does Jesus say will happen to those who refuse to be part of God's kingdom?

Jesus Demonstrates God's Kingdom

Jesus did more than just teach about God's kingdom. He also demonstrated what life in the kingdom of God is like. Throughout Jesus' ministry, he performed what we call *miracles*—acts that cannot be explained through natural means—to demonstrate God's kingdom power on earth. Jesus frequently stepped into the chaos of this broken world to make things right. We find one example of this in the following story told in the Gospel of John:

> ¹ *Some time later, Jesus went up to Jerusalem for one of the Jewish festivals.* ² *Now there is in Jerusalem near the Sheep Gate a pool, which in Aramaic is called Bethesda and which is surrounded by five covered colonnades.* ³ *Here a great number of disabled people used to lie—the blind, the lame, the para-lyzed.* [4] ⁵ *One who was there had been an invalid for thirty-eight years.* ⁶ *When Jesus saw him lying there and learned that he had been in this con-dition for a long time, he asked him, "Do you want to get well?"*
>
> ⁷ *"Sir," the invalid replied, "I have no one to help me into the pool when the water is stirred. While I am trying to get in, someone else goes down ahead of me."*
>
> ⁸ *Then Jesus said to him, "Get up! Pick up your mat and walk."* ⁹ *At once the man was cured; he picked up his mat and walked.*
>
> John 5:1–9

In this story, Jesus demonstrated his power over disease and sickness. He healed a man who had been lame for thirty-eight years and spent his days sitting beside a pool hoping for a miracle. Jesus said him, "Get up! Pick up your mat and walk" (verse

8). This was a bold thing to say to someone who hadn't walked in nearly four decades. But here, Jesus was revealing his authority over sickness and disease by taking something broken and making it right.

Jesus performed many other acts of healing like this throughout his ministry. He healed the son of an official who was close to death (see John 4:46–54). He healed his disciple Peter's mother-in-law of a fever (see Mark 1:29–31). He healed a man who was afflicted with leprosy (see Mark 1:40–45), a man who had been blind since birth (see John 9:1–7), and a man who was deaf (see Mark 7:31–37). Jesus demonstrated the power of God's kingdom by speaking to a storm to cause it to cease (see Mark 4:35–41). He revealed God's authority over Satan by casting an "impure spirit" (a demon) out of a boy (see Luke 9:37–43).

In all these stories—and many others in the Gospels—the one who spoke all things into existence speaks and shows his authority over the physical world. But perhaps the greatest miracle of all, outside of Jesus' resurrection, is told in John 11. We touched on this story briefly in a previous lesson, but to set up the scene, Jesus' friend Lazarus had just died. Jesus wept, knowing sin had brought this reality into his perfect world, and then acts:

> [38] *Jesus, once more deeply moved, came to the tomb. It was a cave with a stone laid across the entrance.* [39] *"Take away the stone," he said.*
>
> *"But, Lord," said Martha, the sister of the dead man, "by this time there is a bad odor, for he has been there four days."*
>
> [40] *Then Jesus said, "Did I not tell you that if you believe, you will see the glory of God?"*
>
> [41] *So they took away the stone. Then Jesus looked up and said, "Father, I thank you that you have heard me.* [42] *I knew that you always hear me, but I said this for the benefit of the people standing here, that they may believe that you sent me."*
>
> [43] *When he had said this, Jesus called in a loud voice, "Lazarus, come out!"* [44] *The dead man came out, his hands and feet wrapped with strips of linen, and a cloth around his face.*
>
> *Jesus said to them, "Take off the grave clothes and let him go."*
>
> John 11:38–44

Jesus has the power over death. He spoke to a corpse and called it to life. Certainly, this is a picture of the spiritual reality of what God does for all those he saves. He calls them from spiritual death to new life in Christ. But we shouldn't miss the concrete reality of the experience of Lazarus. He was dead—smelly dead. There was no mistaking the reality of the moment, yet Jesus remained undeterred. He walked to the tomb, spoke to the dead man, and called him to life. Because Jesus' words have power, even the then-dead Lazarus responded to his call and came out of the tomb alive, grave clothes and all.

These acts are surely "miraculous." But more fundamentally, they are demonstrations of the kingdom of God. They are Jesus showing us what the kingdom is like. They represent his work of taking something broken and making it whole—taking something wrong and making it right. Whole we don't get to see the kingdom of God arrive in full force, as the people of Jesus' day expected, we do get a peek into what we can expect. God's kingdom is like a bright light covered by a paper bag in a dark room, and the miracles of Jesus are like little pinpricks in that bag. Little rays of light begin to burst through and create brilliant displays on the walls.

Jesus once said of his ministry on earth, "The blind receive sight, the lame walk, those who have leprosy are cleansed, the deaf hear, the dead are raised, and the good news is proclaimed to the poor. Blessed is anyone who does not stumble on account of me" (Matthew 11:5-6). Jesus was pointing out these glimpses of God's kingdom in his earthly ministry. His miracles were a way of saying, "See, this is what heaven is like!" Storms don't rage in heaven—there, creation declares God's beauty in glorious splendor. Sickness doesn't exist in heaven—there, people have new bodies freed from the ravishes of disease and age. Death is no more in heaven—there, life abundant is on display, and will be for all eternity.

7. How did Jesus demonstrate God's power over disease in the healing of the man in John 5:1-8? What did this miracle reveal about Jesus' authority?

8. In John 11:38–44, was the point of Jesus' miracle about Lazarus being healed, or restoring the faith of Lazarus' friends, or both? Explain your response.

REFLECT

Jesus taught and demonstrated that the kingdom of God had come and then continually invited those with "ears to hear" (Mark 4:9) enter into the kingdom and be saved. Jesus taught them what it was like to live under his rule in the new kingdom that he was bringing to earth. In the Sermon on the Mount, he announced God's blessing that had come to those in his kingdom and then described the life those kingdom citizens could live. He called them to be salt and light in the world by bringing the good news to bear in the world (see Matthew 5:13–16).

Jesus commended love in contrast to anger, beauty in contrast to lust, and truth in contrast to deception (see 5:21–37). He invited kingdom citizens to love others, even their enemies, knowing that God demonstrated love for his enemies by sending his Son (see 5:38–48). He reminded them to show generosity to the poor (see 6:1–4), to pray and fast passionately (see 6:5–18), to avoid attachment to temporal trinkets on this earth (see 6:19–24), and to trust God to meet their needs (Matthew 6:25–34).

Each theme is a reminder of heaven. God calls his kingdom citizens to live this way as a picture of heaven coming to earth. When they forgive and love their enemies, they do so as a signpost pointing to the heavenly forgiveness that God's people experience in heaven. When they relinquish a death-grip on materialism and invest in God's work in the world, they point forward to the world that will last long after the possessions of this earth decay.

It's easy for us to read these commands today as a list of entrance requirements to get into the kingdom of God. Seen in that light, it seems like a lofty set of rules that we intuitively know are out of our reach. But that is not what Jesus had in mind. He wasn't suggesting rules that are necessary to merit the kingdom. Instead, he was calling those he has saved to a distinctively kingdom-informed and kingdom-infused life. He wants his people, as kingdom citizens, to model heavenly realities through their earthly lives.

9. In what ways does God continue to show us what his kingdom is like today?

10. How have you seen evidence of heaven coming to earth in your own life?

CLOSE

Jesus' life told the story of God's kingdom. There is certainly much about his day-to-day activities that we don't know because they were not written down. But the Bible preserves an authoritative picture of what God deemed to be most important. Jesus showed people the kingdom of God through his life and pointed the way for them to become a part of it.

This is the same mission for all who bear Jesus' name and call themselves his followers. We are called to spend our days showing people the kingdom of God through acts of love, mercy, compassion, and kindness. We are to tell others about the availability of the kingdom of God by pointing them to the good news of what Jesus has done to save sinners and restore the world. As the Father sent Jesus into the world, so all disciples are sent into the world (see John 17:18; 20:21). We go, seeking to spend our lives the way Jesus did. All the while declaring, "I have brought you glory on earth by finishing the work you gave me to do" (John 17:4).

11. How does the obedience of God's people help others see the beauty of God's love? How does it give them a picture of what heaven will be like?

12. What are some practical ways you are able to share God's love with others this week?

Lesson Five

SAVED

But he was pierced for our transgressions, he was crushed for our iniquities; the punishment that brought us peace was on him, and by his wounds we are healed.

ISAIAH 53:5

God made him who had no sin to be sin for us, so that in him we might become the righteousness of God.

2 CORINTHIANS 5:21

For it is by
grace you have
been saved,
through faith.

EPHESIANS 2:8

WELCOME

Going back to my basketball days, I remember there was usually one player on the team who would struggle most days. He simply could not do what the coach was asking him to do on time. It was a pitiful sight. The poor soul would be out on the court running wind sprints while the rest of us watched. At some point, the coach would step in and show mercy. However, he would not show mercy by just letting the offender off the hook. No, his mercy was tied to a sacrifice.

The coach would give the team a choice. Either the struggling player could keep running, or the rest of us could take his place by doing ten more wind sprints on his behalf. Of course, we would always (though begrudgingly) choose to run for our teammate. We did this not only because we cared for the player but also because we knew there would come a day when we would struggle in our conditioning and need our teammates to fill in for us.

We all need a substitute from time to time—a person to fill in a shift for us at work, someone to run an errand in our place, a friend to jump in to take the lead on a project. We need the assurance that someone is there to take the baton from us when we need a break. When we are at the end of what we can do on our own, we need someone to step up and help.

As we discussed in a previous lesson, when it comes to living up to God's standard for our lives, we will all fall short every time. God's measure by which he judges us is holiness and perfection, and we simply cannot measure up to it. As Solomon lamented, "There is no one on earth who is righteous, no one who does what is right and never sins" (Ecclesiastes 7:20). Therefore, someone had to take our place. Jesus had to come to earth because, ultimately, he is the only who could physically stand in our place through his death on the cross.

In the Old Testament, the way God's people restored their relationship with him was through a physical sacrifice. The system required the blood of an animal to be spilled. A simple demonstration would not suffice. Just saying, "I'm sorry, I won't do it again," would not do the trick. No, God decreed that a living creature without blemish had to stand in for the guilty party (see Leviticus 4:32–35). Blood was the currency of forgiveness.

This is why Jesus had to be both divine and human. In his divinity, he could lead a perfect life without sin. In his humanity, he could physically stand in for sinful humanity. The Bible states that "God made him who had no sin to be sin for us, so that in him we might become the righteousness of God" (2 Corinthians 5:21). As the theologian and reformer John Calvin noted, "The Son of God, the spotlessly pure, took upon him the disgrace and ignominy of our iniquities, and in return clothes us with his purity."

Jesus was our substitute. Theologians use the word *propitiation* to describe what he did on our behalf—a big word that just means he took the place in which we were meant to stand. Due to our sin, we deserved death, wrath, and judgment. But Jesus physically took that on himself. Seeing Jesus standing in our place helps us to believe that he is our Savior.

1. What would you change in your life if you know how and when you were going to die?

2. What do you feel when you think about the fact that Jesus sacrificed himself for you?

READ

You can learn a lot about a person by the way he or she approaches death. Our hearts are warmed when we read stories of elderly married couples who die days apart. We celebrate the heroism of those who rescue others from a tragic accident, only to lose their own lives in the process. The love or bravery exemplified in these stories characterizes a life well-lived.

But the nature of our death is always uncertain. Sure, people can anticipate the possibility of death when they go into high-risk environments such as firefighting or military combat, but they do not know for sure if and when they are going to die. We can only hope the character that we have built over a lifetime will be on display whenever that moment arrives.

This is what makes it difficult for us when it comes to wrapping our minds around Jesus' story. As we have discussed throughout this study, Jesus was fully God and fully man, sent on a mission to save sinners and restore the world. Because he is God, he has always known the plan from the outset, including the way that his earthly life would come to a close.

The Old Testament pointed toward the eventual sacrifice of Jesus. Initially, as we have noted, animal sacrifices offered at the temple were God's method of reconciliation for the people. However, the prophet Isaiah indicated that one day those sacrifices would be replaced by something far greater, as the following passages relate:

> [2] *He grew up before him like a tender shoot,*
> *and like a root out of dry ground.*
> *He had no beauty or majesty to attract us to him,*
> *nothing in his appearance that we should desire him.*
> [3] *He was despised and rejected by mankind,*
> *a man of suffering, and familiar with pain.*
> *Like one from whom people hide their faces*
> *he was despised, and we held him in low esteem.*
>
> [4] *Surely he took up our pain*
> *and bore our suffering,*

yet we considered him punished by God,
stricken by him, and afflicted.
[5] *But he was pierced for our transgressions,*
he was crushed for our iniquities;
the punishment that brought us peace was on him,
and by his wounds we are healed.
[6] *We all, like sheep, have gone astray,*
each of us has turned to our own way;
and the Lord has laid on him
the iniquity of us all. . . .

[10] *Yet it was the Lord's will to crush him and cause him to suffer,*
and though the Lord makes his life an offering for sin,
he will see his offspring and prolong his days,
and the will of the Lord will prosper in his hand.

Isaiah 53:2–6, 10

We know that Jesus was aware of how his life would end because he started talking about his death long before it happened. One time, after helping his disciples understand that he was God's Messiah, he pointed forward to his coming death by saying, "The Son of Man must suffer many things and be rejected by the elders, the chief priests and the teachers of the law, and he must be killed and on the third day be raised to life" (Luke 9:22).

At the end of that same chapter, Jesus again told his disciples that he would soon be given into the hands of men and put to death (see verse 44). This was not some vague premonition that his death was coming. Jesus was not merely pointing to what he thought might happen. Rather, he knew exactly how and when his death was going to go down. He knew all the horrific agony that awaited him. He knew about the cross.

We might assume this knowledge would have changed the way Jesus lived. After all, if we knew that we were going to die a tragic death, wouldn't we work to avoid that presumed outcome? We would certainly avoid the places and people that seemed likely to bring us harm. But not so with Jesus. Immediately after (twice) predicating that he was going to be killed, we read, "Jesus resolutely set out for Jerusalem" (Luke 9:51).

Jerusalem was the one place for certain that Jesus should not have gone if he was hoping to escape his fate. It was the place where the Jewish religious leaders were meeting to plot his death. And plot they did, as the following story relates:

> [1] *When Jesus had finished saying all these things, he said to his disciples,* [2] *"As you know, the Passover is two days away—and the Son of Man will be handed over to be crucified."*
> [3] *Then the chief priests and the elders of the people assembled in the palace of the high priest, whose name was Caiaphas,* [4] *and they schemed to arrest Jesus secretly and kill him.* [5] *"But not during the festival," they said, "or there may be a riot among the people."*
>
> Matthew 26:1–5

We read these words and think, *No, Jesus! Not Jerusalem! That is where the religious leaders live. Didn't you hear what you yourself just said? They are going to kill you!* Jesus was not ignorant or forgetful. He knew what awaited him in Jerusalem . . . and he went there anyway. We learn a lot about Jesus from the way he approached his own death.

3. What did the prophecy in Isaiah 53:2–6, 10 reveal about the nature of the Messiah's death? What does God say he would "place" on the Messiah?

4. What did Jesus understand about his mission? How did this enable him to decide to go to Jerusalem—even though he knew what awaited him there?

REFLECT

Jesus Had the End in Mind

The author of Hebrews gives us Jesus' rationale for going to the cross: "For the joy set before him he endured the cross, scorning its shame, and sat down at the right hand of the throne of God" (Hebrews 12:2). Jesus was able to go to Jerusalem, and ultimately to the cross, because he knew the "joy" that awaited him. He knew the end from the beginning. He understood the cross would not have the final word. His death would accomplish the salvation of God's people, and ultimately he would return to the Father in his full glory. So he went to the cross.

Jesus, in one of his messages directed at the religious leaders, said that he was the Good Shepherd (see John 10:11–18). This is an image used throughout the Old Testament to describe God and his care for his people (see Psalm 80:1; Ezekiel 34:23; Micah 5:4). Jesus was saying that he, as the Good Shepherd, would not merely care for his sheep by feeding and leading them—he would go as far as laying down his life for the sheep whom he loves.

Jesus also wanted the religious leaders to know that he was willingly laying down his life. He said, "The reason my Father loves me is that I lay down my life—only to take it up again. No one takes it from me, but I lay it down of my own accord. I have authority to lay it down and authority to take it up again" (John 10:17–18). Jesus was not a mere pawn in the plans of the religious leaders of his day. He was not some helpless zealot who suffered a martyr's death. He was—and is—the eternal God who created all things and gave his life for us.

5. It seems counterintuitive that Jesus would endure the pain of the cross for the "joy" set before him. But what did Jesus know his death would accomplish?

6. What was Jesus saying to the religious authorities by claiming to be the Good Shepherd? Why is it important that Jesus willingly gave up his life for our sins?

Jesus Accomplished Reconciliation at the Cross

The death of Jesus was the primary focus of all who wrote about his life. For instance, the Gospel writer Mark spent no time describing Jesus' birth but instead chose to focus half of his writing on the days surrounding Jesus' death. The other Gospel writers followed a similar pattern, devoting extensive chapters to describing the arrest, mock trial, and ultimately the crucifixion of Jesus. Paul would later relate why this was the case: "For what I received I passed on to you as of first importance: that Christ died for our sins according to the Scriptures, that he was buried, that he was raised on the third day according to the Scriptures" (1 Corinthians 15:3–4).

Paul also told the Corinthian church that the purpose of his letter was to remind them that this truth was of primary importance (see verses 1–2). He could have gone on to mention Jesus' extraordinary birth. He could have described the miracles that stunned onlookers and changed people's lives. He could have summarized Jesus' teachings. But that is not what Paul did. Instead, he wrote that what was of first importance was the death, burial, and resurrection of Christ. And that is what makes the good news really good news indeed.

In Paul's second letter to the Corinthians, he summarized why this aspect of Jesus' life was such a big deal: "All this is from God, who reconciled us to himself through Christ and gave us the ministry of reconciliation: that God was reconciling the world to himself in Christ, not counting people's sins against them. And he has committed to us the message of reconciliation. We are therefore Christ's ambassadors, as though God were making his appeal through us. We implore you on Christ's behalf: Be reconciled to God" (2 Corinthians 5:18–20).

Paul uses the image of reconciliation to describe what Jesus accomplished on the cross. While we may not use the word *reconciliation* in everyday conversation, it is a common idea. The picture is that of taking two people who were once enemies and making them friends again. A reconciled relationship is one that was broken and has now been made right.

7.   Why did the Gospel writers focus so much of their narratives on the arrest, mock trial, and crucifixion of Jesus? What were they emphasizing to their readers?

8.   What does Paul say in 2 Corinthians 5:18–20 that Jesus accomplished for us at the cross? What has God, in turn, committed to us?

Jesus Provided the Way to Righteousness

As we have discussed in this study, the relationship between God and people had been broken because of sin. All people were God's enemies, rebelling against him and despising his love. Jesus' death changed that dynamic. He reconciled people to God through a great exchange. Jesus lived a perfect life and died a sinner's death. He now offers us both life and righteousness.

First, we can exchange his death for ours by believing in faith that he died in our place. This is what Peter was communicating when he wrote, "For Christ also suffered once for sins, the righteous for the unrighteous, to bring you to God" (1 Peter 3:18). The Righteous One suffered the death the unrighteous deserved because of their sins. If there were any doubt as to the hideous nature of sin, we need only look at the way Jesus died to understand how bad it is. Jesus was brutally mocked, tortured, and killed in the most excruciating way known to man. There were few deaths more painful than death on a Roman cross. But this is just what Jesus endured for those he loved. It was the death we all deserved—and Jesus took it in our place.

But that is not all that Jesus did for us. Paul tells us that Jesus also made a way for us to obtain God's righteousness: "God made him who had no sin to be sin for us, so that in him we might become the righteousness of God" (2 Corinthians 5:21). Here again, *righteousness* is not a word we use every day, but it simply means we gain the perfection of God—his holiness. People are clearly not righteous before God. They are marred and broken in sin. So how could they stand before a God who is holy and pure? The answer is Jesus.

Jesus gives us his righteousness as a gift. He lived a perfect life—the very life that every other person who came before him was incapable of living. Jesus succeeded where everyone else failed. Therefore, he has all righteousness and can give it to whomever he saves. This reality provides great hope for all who know themselves to be sinners in need of grace.

Paul explains this process using the imagery of getting dressed, stating that those who have been saved are now "clothed" in the righteousness of Christ (Galatians 3:27). When God now looks at us, he sees only his perfect Son. Not only are our sins paid for through Jesus' death, but also God sees us as righteous and holy before him. Of us he says, "I will forgive their wickedness and will remember their sins no more" (Hebrews 8:12).

God hasn't forgotten our sins, but because of Jesus, he chooses not to remember them or hold them against us now or in the future. He says to us, "This is the covenant I will make with them after that time. . . . I will put my laws in their hearts, and

I will write them on their minds. . . . Their sins and lawless acts I will remember no more" (Hebrews 10:16–17).

9. Jesus reconciled people to God through a "great exchange"—his life for our own. How does the fact that Jesus did this cause you to love and worship him?

10. Jesus has enabled us to be "clothed" in God's righteousness. What comes to mind when you consider that when God now looks at you, he sees only his perfect Son?

CLOSE

Jesus' death was the purpose of his life. As we have learned, he knew from birth that he would give his life on the cross. The fact that he did reveals that he understood his death to be the very purpose for which he was sent. He was God's promised Savior—the one pledged to crush Satan, sin, and death from Genesis 3 onward. Each of us who have been saved by his grace have been made a part of this great story that God is writing in human history.

Because of the sacrifice that Jesus made for us, we can have hope, even though we don't know how our lives will end or when we will die. We can know the ultimate outcome that awaits us. Death will not have the final answer for those who are in Christ because he faced death on our behalf. As Christians, we can face uncertain death with confidence, knowing the great exchange paid the price for our sins and gave us a right standing before God.

But there is one more step to consider in this glorious process: Jesus didn't stay dead. His resurrection and ascension changed everything, validating he was who he said he was and has done what he promised to do. It is to this subject that we turn in the final week of this study.

11. How does Jesus' sacrifice give you hope today?

12. What are some tangible things you can do this week to live in light of this truth?

Lesson Six

ALIVE

*Then the L*ORD *said to Moses,*
"I will rain down bread from heaven for you."

EXODUS 16:4

Mary Magdalene went to the disciples with the news:
"I have seen the Lord!" And she told them that he had
said these things to her.

JOHN 20:18

God raised the

Lord from the

dead, and he will

raise us also.

1 CORINTHIANS 6:14

WELCOME

When Carmen and I were starting churches in New York City, one of the congregations met near the Empire State Building. You could get a perfect view of the iconic skyscraper from the roof where we were meeting. We had a young couple in the church who had been dating for several months, and the man wanted to ask his girlfriend to marry him. He approached me about using the roof of the building for the occasion. He had it all planned out—a nice romantic dinner complete with music and the illuminating glow of the Empire State Building.

It was an incredible scene. He had also arranged for all their friends to gather downstairs in the main part of the building for an after-party. About sixty people were gathered, anticipating the couple's descent from the rooftop. Everyone, especially the ladies, was dying to hear every detail of the proposal. *What did he say? What song was played? How did she like the setting?* They wanted to hear everything.

After about ninety minutes on the roof, the couple emerged, and we all went crazy with excitement. The bride-to-be was brimming with joy. She worked the room, recounting every single event of the last hour and half. She led with her left hand extended so that everyone could get a good view of the ring. No detail was spared.

Here is the amazing thing about that night: no one had to motivate the couple to share their good news. No one had to say, "Come on, now, tell us all about it." No one had to beg them to recount the events on the roof. No, they shared it naturally. It would have been strange—and a bad sign—if the couple had refused to talk about what they just experienced.

Why do I tell this story? Because we share good news naturally. Think about this in your own life. Have you ever won a big prize? Received an unexpected job promotion?

Maybe experienced the birth of a child? If so, you likely you did not have a problem telling anyone about it. No one had come to you and give you a ten-step program for sharing the news. You didn't need someone to prompt you to spill all the details. No, you just shared that good news with others naturally.

Those who witnessed Jesus' miraculous power likewise did not need to be prompted to share what they had seen. In Mark 5:1–20, we read of a man who was in a desperate situation. He had come to be possessed by a legion of demons, and he was now living away from his community among the tombs. The people had tried to contain him by chaining him to the rocks, but he tore the chains apart and broke the irons on his feet. Day and night he would cry out and cut himself with stones. There was seemingly no hope for this man.

But then Jesus entered his story! He had compassion on this man, even asking his name, and then cast out the demons into a herd of pigs. When the people of the town came to see what was causing all the commotion, they found the man dressed and "in his right mind" (verse 15). Jesus then told the man to "go home to your people and tell them how much the Lord has done for you" (verse 19). So the man went away and began to tell everyone in the Decapolis (ten cities east of the Sea of Galilee) what Jesus had done for him.

No one needed to prompt the man to tell his story. He just naturally shared the good news of what had happened to him. It was a story that he willingly wanted to share. The same would be true of the events that would happen a short time later, when Jesus broke the bounds of death and rose from the grave. It was a story the followers of Jesus couldn't stop telling.

1. What is some good news that you have recently been able to share with others? Did you find that it was easy or difficult to share the good news?

2. What do you think made it so easy for the former demon-possessed man to share what Jesus had done for him throughout the Decapolis?

READ

All Hope Appears to Be Gone

It would have been fascinating to be a bystander when the news first circulated that Jesus had risen from the dead. Today, we read about Jesus' resurrection in the Bible and quickly move on to the next story. We are familiar with it—at least from a conceptual level. So when we hear about someone who was dead coming back to life, it does not stop us in our tracks.

But this was certainly not the experience of those who knew and loved Jesus Christ. They had staked all their hopes for the future on the one they knew as the Messiah. They loved and shared life with him. Many had experienced the personal transformation that his presence brought with it. They had been healed, vindicated, and forgiven. Their affection for Jesus wasn't mere appreciation—their lives had been changed because he was in them.

But then, suddenly, he wasn't. He was dead. Gone . . . seemingly forever. Those who went to the tomb that first Easter morning were not expecting to find it empty. For them, it must have felt that all hope was lost—that everything Jesus had promised was not going to come to pass. Even those who went to the tomb and found it empty (like Mary Magdalene) just assumed that someone had stolen his body. They did not believe that he had risen from the dead.

In the Old Testament, we are reminded of times when the people of God likewise lost their hope. They believed circumstances were going to go one way, but then their current situation led them to believe the exact opposite was going to happen. One example is found in the story of the children of Israel wandering in the wilderness after escaping bondage in Egypt. As the following passage relates, it didn't take long for them to lose their hope in God:

> [1] *The whole Israelite community set out from Elim and came to the Desert of Sin, which is between Elim and Sinai, on the fifteenth day of the second month after they had come out of Egypt.* [2] *In the desert the whole community grumbled against Moses and Aaron.* [3] *The Israelites said to them, "If only we had died by the LORD's hand in Egypt! There we sat around pots of meat and ate all the food we wanted, but you have brought us out into this desert to starve this entire assembly to death."*
>
> [4] *Then the LORD said to Moses, "I will rain down bread from heaven for you. The people are to go out each day and gather enough for that day. In this way I will test them and see whether they will follow my instructions.* [5] *On the sixth day they are to prepare what they bring in, and that is to be twice as much as they gather on the other days."*
>
> Exodus 16:1–5

Losing faith causes us to think drastically. The people of Israel were wishing they had died in Egypt rather than be subject to the harsh conditions of the desert. They had lost sight of God's promise and were caught up in their current predicament. The same was initially true for the early arrivals at the tomb. But soon their tone would shift dramatically.

3. The Israelites had witnessed the miraculous power of God in their deliverance from Egypt. So why do you think they were so quick to lose faith in God?

4. What kind of "drastic thinking" did the people exhibit in their distress? How did God reveal that in spite of their faithlessness, he was still faithful to them?

A Promise Comes True

When we look at the account of Jesus' resurrection, we can't overlook the fact that Jesus had told his disciples that it was going to happen. In the Gospel of Mark we find Jesus foretelling his resurrection on three separate occasions (see Mark 8:31–33; 9:30–32; 10:32–34). But who would have thought it would happen? People who die stay dead. It is just the way it works.

Sure, we would like to believe that our loved ones could come back to life, but we know those hopes will not be realized. The same was certainly true for Jesus' friends. They had seen other friends and family die. So why would they think things would be different with Jesus?

Of course, in reality, they had every reason to believe that things would be different with Jesus. Everything was different with Jesus. Nothing that he said or did was "normal," at least according to a human way of thinking. And everything that Jesus said was going to happen came true. So when Jesus spoke of a coming resurrection, his disciples should have been listening. Still, as the following stories relate, the followers of Jesus were caught off guard:

> [1] *After the Sabbath, at dawn on the first day of the week, Mary Magdalene and the other Mary went to look at the tomb. . . .* [5] *The angel said to the women, "Do not be afraid, for I know that you are looking for Jesus, who was crucified.* [6] *He is not here; he has risen, just as he said. Come and see the place where he lay.* [7] *Then go quickly and tell his disciples: 'He has risen from the dead and is going ahead of you into Galilee. There you will see him.' Now I have told you."*
>
> Matthew 28:1–7

¹ On the first day of the week, very early in the morning, the women took the spices they had prepared and went to the tomb. ² They found the stone rolled away from the tomb, ³ but when they entered, they did not find the body of the Lord Jesus. ⁴ While they were wondering about this, suddenly two men in clothes that gleamed like lightning stood beside them. ⁵ In their fright the women bowed down with their faces to the ground, but the men said to them, "Why do you look for the living among the dead? ⁶ He is not here; he has risen! Remember how he told you, while he was still with you in Galilee: ⁷ 'The Son of Man must be delivered over to the hands of sinners, be crucified and on the third day be raised again.'" ⁸ Then they remembered his words.

Luke 24:1–8

¹ Early on the first day of the week, while it was still dark, Mary Magdalene went to the tomb and saw that the stone had been removed from the entrance. ² So she came running to Simon Peter and the other disciple, the one Jesus loved, and said, "They have taken the Lord out of the tomb, and we don't know where they have put him!"³ So Peter and the other disciple started for the tomb. . . . ⁶ Simon Peter came along behind him and went straight into the tomb. He saw the strips of linen lying there, ⁷ as well as the cloth that had been wrapped around Jesus' head. The cloth was still lying in its place, separate from the linen. ⁸ Finally the other disciple, who had reached the tomb first, also went inside. He saw and believed. ⁹ (They still did not understand from Scripture that Jesus had to rise from the dead.) ¹⁰ Then the disciples went back to where they were staying.

John 20:1–3, 6–10

5. In Matthew 28:6 and Luke 24:6–7, what did the angelic beings remind Jesus' followers that he had said? Why do you think they found it so hard to believe Jesus' words?

6. What does John 20:2 reveal about what Mary Magdalene thought had happened to Jesus? What did Peter believe (see verse 6) when he saw the empty tomb?

Believers and Doubters

In the story of the Israelites told in Exodus 16:1–5, the people's outlook began to change when the Lord sent a sign of his provision. In the midst of their frustration and lack of faith, God promised to rain down "bread from heaven" as a physical manifestation of his presence with them. The same was true of the disciples at the empty tomb when the angel (or angels) announced that Jesus had risen. It completely changed their outlook. We see this particularly in the Gospel of John, where one follower actually encountered the risen Christ:

> [11] *Now Mary stood outside the tomb crying. As she wept, she bent over to look into the tomb* [12] *and saw two angels in white, seated where Jesus' body had been, one at the head and the other at the foot.*
>
> [13] *They asked her, "Woman, why are you crying?"*
>
> *"They have taken my Lord away," she said, "and I don't know where they have put him."* [14] *At this, she turned around and saw Jesus standing there, but she did not realize that it was Jesus.*
>
> [15] *He asked her, "Woman, why are you crying? Who is it you are looking for?"*
>
> *Thinking he was the gardener, she said, "Sir, if you have carried him away, tell me where you have put him, and I will get him."*
>
> [16] *Jesus said to her, "Mary."*
>
> *She turned toward him and cried out in Aramaic, "Rabboni!" (which means "Teacher").*
>
> [17] *Jesus said, "Do not hold on to me, for I have not yet ascended to the Father. Go instead to my brothers and tell them, 'I am ascending to my Father and your Father, to my God and your God.'"*

¹⁸ Mary Magdalene went to the disciples with the news: "I have seen the Lord!" And she told them that he had said these things to her.

John 20:11–18

In this story, Mary captures the essence of the good news when she proclaims, "I have seen the Lord!" (verse 18). Her words are multifaceted. Sure, she is saying that she has seen Jesus, the Lord, in the flesh. But more than that, she is now convinced without a doubt that he is the Lord. He is exactly who he proclaimed to be all the time that he was with them. He is the King of kings and Lord of lords. There was simply no doubt for her after the resurrection.

But there were those who still doubted! One such follower now has a nickname attached to his disbelief. "Doubting" Thomas, as he came to be known, was not present when Jesus appeared to the rest of the disciples shortly after appearing to Mary (see verses 19–23). As a result, he said, "Unless I see the nail marks in his hands and put my finger where the nails were, and put my hand into his side, I will not believe (verse 25). Here is what happened next:

²⁶ A week later his disciples were in the house again, and Thomas was with them. Though the doors were locked, Jesus came and stood among them and said, "Peace be with you!" ²⁷ Then he said to Thomas, "Put your finger here; see my hands. Reach out your hand and put it into my side. Stop doubting and believe."

²⁸ Thomas said to him, "My Lord and my God!"

²⁹ Then Jesus told him, "Because you have seen me, you have believed; blessed are those who have not seen and yet have believed."

John 20:26–29

Thomas had to see and touch Jesus' nail-scared body for him to believe, but when he did, the same shout of praise resulted: "My Lord and my God!" (verse 28). Thomas saw and believed.

There are still many today who doubt Jesus. They doubt who he said he was and doubt that he actually rose from the dead. Fast-forward some 2,000 years, and it's still jarring to think that a man could be born who was fully God . . . and that this

God-man would then give his life to take the place of those he loves . . . and that this very same God-man would overcome death by rising again. Such claims take great faith to believe. However, the kind of faith to which Jesus calls us to is actually not unlike the type of faith that we employ in our everyday lives.

7. How did Mary Magdalene's outlook change when she heard Jesus say her name? Why do you think this encounter convinced her that Jesus had truly risen?

8. What did Thomas say was required for him to believe that Jesus had risen from the dead? How did Jesus meet Thomas where he was—in his doubt?

REFLECT

Faith is rational belief—trust that acts without every detail being visible. It takes faith to get on an airplane and sit calmly while it glides at 30,000 feet. It takes faith to swipe a plastic card through a kiosk at a store to buy some groceries. We live by faith anytime we love another person, believing that he or she is faithful and committed to the relationship. Certainly, there are times when our faith proves unjustified, but that is because the object of our faith proves faulty, not because we should not have employed faith in the first place. The reality is that life is impossible to live apart from faith. We couldn't function if it were not for faith.

The type of faith that Jesus requires is different than these examples, but it is also far more dependable. The faithfulness of Jesus is the key to our faith, because faith hinges on the dependability of the object of faith. A plane is as trustworthy as the quality of its pilot. A relationship is as trustworthy as each person in it. A Savior is as trustworthy as his character. The trustworthy character of God is a consistent theme throughout the Bible. There were times in Israel's history when it seemed unlikely that God would be able to keep his promises to his people, but each time he came through. He did exactly what he said he would do.

If God has proven that he can be trusted, it only stands to reason that we should trust in him and in Jesus as our Savior. We trust that he lived the life that we should have lived and given us his righteousness as a gift. We trust that he has paid the penalty for our sin. We trust that his resurrection is a foretaste of our own.

Paul describes this reality in 1 Corinthians 15:21-23: "For since death came through a man, the resurrection of the dead comes also through a man. For as in Adam all die, so in Christ all will be made alive. But each in turn: Christ, the firstfruits; then, when he comes, those who belong to him." This picture of firstfruits is telling. It pictures the first produce from the harvest. The initial intake means that there is more on the way. A generous harvest is likely if the firstfruits are plentiful.

Jesus is the "firstfruits." He is not the only one who will experience resurrection—so will all who trust him in faith. His victory over sin and death will belong to them as well. They will receive new bodies that will no longer show the signs of death and decay. They will spend eternity in a world free from sin, just like Jesus. All that is his will be theirs as a gift of his grace. In a world of bad news, Jesus gives us overwhelming good news. It is the kind of news that changes everything. What makes it even better is that it is the kind of good news that none of us deserves or can earn. It comes to us as an inheritance based on someone else's work.

Imagine a recent college graduate who learns of his beloved grandfather's death. The young man loves his grandfather and grieves his passing. He is then stunned to learn that his grandfather was incredibly wealthy—he had worked hard, earned well, saved diligently, and invested strategically. As a result, there is now a significant inheritance awaiting him—all of which the young man had done nothing to earn. Someone else had earned it for him. All the grandson needed was a relationship with his grandfather—and all that he had was his.

The same is true with Jesus. He did the heavy lifting to earn God's reward, and he gives this inheritance to his people. Paul writes that he has qualified us "to share in the inheritance of his holy people in the kingdom of light" (Colossians 1:12). He also describes the "riches of his glorious inheritance" (Ephesians 1:18) that awaits those who put their faith in him. Jesus is rich in all the ways that matter and, as an act of grace, gives that inheritance to his people.

But there is an important facet to mention here. Much like the grandson, a relationship is essential for claiming this inheritance. Jesus once told a parable in which God separated the "sheep" (those who are his) from the "goats" (those who are not). To the group of sheep, he said, "Come, you who are blessed . . . take your inheritance, the kingdom prepared for you since the creation of the world" (Matthew 25:34). These words are our only hope in this life and the next. No one—and nothing else—can give an inheritance like God can. Only he has a kingdom prepared for us from before the creation of the world that can be ours by faith.

9. What is something you do every day that requires an act of faith on your part?

10. What inheritance have you been given in Christ? Why is it essential to have a relationship with Christ in order to secure all the blessings that he has for you?

CLOSE

As you close this study, if you are uncertain of your relationship with God, you can—right now—trust in Jesus by placing your faith in him. Simply talk with him in prayer, asking him to forgive you from your sins and save you. If possible, have a conversation with a friend who follows Jesus. Tell that person about what you sense God doing in your life and ask him or her pray with you and walk with you in the days ahead.

For those of you who are already followers of Jesus, allow your deep affection and praise for all that he has done to burn in your heart. Worship him for all that he is and what he has given to you as a gift. Finally, find someone who is far from God, but close to you, and seek out a conversation about the life-changing realities of Jesus' life, death, and resurrection.

It was this recognition of all that God had done that compelled the apostles in the early church to talk so about the death and resurrection of Jesus. Beginning in Acts 1, they understood their responsibility as those who had become "a witness . . . of his resurrection" (verse 22). So they talked about God's work in Christ's resurrection at Pentecost (see 2:24, 32), at the temple (see 3:15, 26), before the Jewish ruling council (see 4:2, 10), and in countless other places. Sharing the good news of the resurrected Jesus wasn't a script they had to learn or a habit they had to develop. For them, the resurrection had really happened, and there was nothing on earth that could stop them from sharing this good news with the world.

11. Why is it important that Jesus not only died for our sins at his crucifixion but also conquered death at his resurrection? Why isn't his death alone enough?

12. What makes the hope you have found in Jesus "good news" for you?

NEXT

In these six lessons of *Savior*, we have seen how God chose to come down to earth in human form and actually dwell among his creation. We looked at how Jesus was both fully divine and fully human—concurrently—and his mission and purpose in coming into this world. We explored what Jesus said about the kingdom of God and how he demonstrated the power of God's kingdom through the many miracles that he performed. Finally, we saw how Jesus offered himself as a sacrifice for the sins of humanity and defeated death at his resurrection.

In *Church*, the next study in *The Jesus Bible Study Series*, we will continue to navigate the story of Jesus' followers after his resurrection and ascension into heaven. We will see how they experienced the power of the Holy Spirit and began to gather into communities to serve one another and share with those who were in need. We will also learn of the persecution they suffered that caused them to scatter . . . taking the good news of Jesus wherever they went. We will see how both Jews and Gentiles alike were eventually able to form a family of brothers and sisters in Christ and how the early believers were called to use their spiritual giftings for others.

Thank you for taking this journey! Stay the course. God has a lot that he wants to do in your life!

LEADER'S GUIDE

Thank you for your willingness to lead your group through this study. What you have chosen to do is valuable and will make a great difference in the lives of others. The rewards of being a leader are different from those of participating, and we hope that as you lead you will find your own walk with Jesus deepened by the experience.

The lessons in this study guide are suitable for church classes, Bible studies, and small groups. Each lesson is structured to provoke thought and help you grow in your knowledge and understanding of Christ. There are multiple components in this section that can help you structure your lessons and discussion time, so make sure you read and consider each one.

BEFORE YOU BEGIN

Before your first meeting, make sure the group members have a copy of this study guide so they can follow along and have their answers written out ahead of time. Alternately, you can hand out the study guides at your first meeting and give the group members some time to look over the material and ask any preliminary questions. During your first meeting, be sure to send a sheet of paper around the room and have the members write down their name, phone number, and email address so you can keep in touch with them during the week.

Generally, the ideal size for a group is eight to ten people, which will ensure that everyone has enough time to participate in discussions. If you have more people, you might want to break up the main group into smaller subgroups. Encourage those who show up at the first meeting to commit to attending the duration of the study. This will help the group members get to know one another, create stability for the group, and help you, as the leader, know how to best prepare each week.

Try to initiate a free-flowing discussion as you go through each lesson. Invite group members to bring any questions they have or insights they discover as they go through the content to the next meeting, especially if they were unsure of the meaning of some parts of the lesson. Be prepared to discuss the biblical truth that relates to each topic in the study.

WEEKLY PREPARATION

As the group leader, here are a few things you can do to prepare for each meeting:

- Make sure you understand the content of the lesson so you know how to structure group time and are prepared to lead group discussion.
- Depending on how much time you have each week, you may not be able to reflect on every question. Select specific questions that you feel will evoke the best discussion.
- At the end of your discussion, take prayer requests from your group members and pray for each other.

STRUCTURING THE DISCUSSION TIME

It is up to you to keep track of the time and keep things on schedule. You might want to set a timer for each question that you discuss so both you and the group members know when your time is up. (There are some good phone apps for timers that play a gentle chime or other pleasant sound instead of a disruptive noise.)

Don't be concerned if the group members are quiet or slow to share. People are often quiet when they are pulling together their ideas, and this might be a new experience for them. Just ask a question and let it hang in the air until someone shares. You can then say, "Thank you. What about others? What thoughts came to you?"

If you need help in organizing your time when planning your group Bible study, the following schedules, for sixty minutes and ninety minutes, can give you a structure for the lesson:

	60 Minutes	90 Minutes
Welcome: Arrive and get settled	5 minutes	10 minutes
Message: Review the lesson	15 minutes	25 minutes
Discussion: Discuss study questions	35 minutes	45 minutes
Prayer: Pray together and dismiss	5 minutes	10 minutes

GROUP DYNAMICS

Leading a group through *Savior* will prove to be highly rewarding both to you and your group members. But you still may encounter challenges along the way! Discussions can get off track. Group members may not be sensitive to the needs and ideas of others. Some might worry they will be expected to talk about matters that make them feel awkward. Others may express comments that result in disagreements. To help ease this strain on you and the group, consider the following ground rules:

- When someone raises a question or comment that is off the main topic, suggest you deal with it another time, or, if you feel led to go in that direction, let the group know you will be spending some time discussing it.

- If someone asks a question that you don't know how to answer, admit it and move on. At your discretion, feel free to invite group members to comment on questions that call for personal experience.

- If you find one or two people are dominating the discussion time, direct a few questions to others in the group. Outside the main group time, ask the more dominating members to help you draw out the quieter ones. Work to make them a part of the solution instead of the problem.

- When a disagreement occurs, encourage the group members to process the matter in love. Encourage those on opposite sides to restate what they heard the other side say about the matter, and then invite each side to evaluate if that perception is accurate. Lead the group in examining other scriptures related to the topic and look for common ground.

When any of these issues arise, encourage your group members to follow these words from the Bible: "Love one another" (John 13:34), "If it is possible, as far as it depends on you, live at peace with everyone" (Romans 12:18), "Whatever is true . . . noble . . . right . . . if anything is excellent or praiseworthy—think about such things" (Philippians 4:8), and "Be quick to listen, slow to speak and slow to become angry" (James 1:19). This will make your group time more rewarding and beneficial for everyone who attends.

Thank you again for your willingness to lead your group. May God reward your efforts and dedication, equip you to guide your group in the weeks ahead, and make your time together fruitful for his kingdom.

ABOUT THE AUTHORS

Aaron Coe has spent more than twenty years working in the non-profit and philanthropic space. Much of that time was spent in New York City in the years after 9/11, helping with revitalization efforts. Aaron served as vice president at North American Mission Board, providing strategic guidance and leadership. He has also worked with organizations like Passion, illumiNations, Food for the Hungry, the Ethics and Religious Liberty Commission, and many others. Aaron has a Ph.D. in Applied Theology and teaches at Dallas Theological Seminary. He is the founder of Future City Now, which seeks to help visionary leaders maximize their influence in the world. Additionally, Aaron served as the General Editor of *The Jesus Bible*. Aaron lives in Atlanta with his wife, Carmen, and their four children.

Matt Rogers holds a Ph.D. in Applied Theology and teaches and writes on Christian mission, ministry, and discipleship. Notably, Matt served as the lead writer for the best-selling *The Jesus Bible*. He and his wife, Sarah, and their five children live in Greenville, South Carolina, where Matt serves as the pastor of Christ Fellowship Cherrydale.

The Jesus Bible Study Series

Beginnings
ISBN 9780310154983
On sale January 2023

Revolt
ISBN 9780310155003
On sale May 2023

People
ISBN 9780310155027
On sale October 2023

Savior
ISBN 9780310155041
On sale January 2024

Church
ISBN 9780310155065
On sale May 2024

Forever
ISBN 9780310155089
On sale September 2024

Available wherever books are sold

 passionpublishing

 HarperChristian Resources

The Jesus Bible

sixty-six books. one story. all about one name.

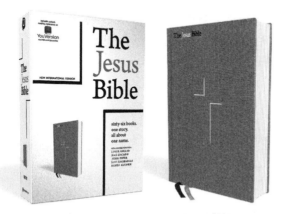

The Jesus Bible, NIV & ESV editions, with feature essays from Louie Giglio, Max Lucado, John Piper, and Randy Alcorn, as well as profound yet accessible study features will help you meet Jesus throughout Scripture.

- 350 full page articles
- 700 side-bar articles
- Book introductions
- Room for journaling

The Jesus Bible Journal, NIV
Study individual books of the Bible featuring lined journal space and commentary from *The Jesus Bible.*

- 14 journals covering 30 books of the Bible
- 2 boxed sets (OT & NT)

TheJesusBible.com

Video Study for Your
Church or Small Group

In this six-session video Bible study, bestselling author and pastor Louie Giglio helps you apply the principles in *Don't Give the Enemy a Seat at Your Table* to your life. The study guide includes access to six streaming video sessions, video notes and a comprehensive structure for group discussion time, and personal study for deeper reflection between sessions.

Study Guide + Streaming Video
9780310156284

DVD
9780310134268

Available now at your favorite bookstore
or streaming video on StudyGateway.com.